SPECTACULAR WINERIES
of Oregon

A CAPTIVATING TOUR OF ESTABLISHED, ESTATE, AND BOUTIQUE WINERIES
Photography by Andréa Johnson

Published by

PANACHE
PANACHE PARTNERS

1424 Gables Court
Plano, TX 75075
469.246.6060
Fax: 469.246.6062
www.panache.com

Publisher: Brian G. Carabet and John Shand

Printed in Malaysia

Distributed by Independent Publishers Group
800.888.4741

PUBLISHER'S DATA

Spectacular Wineries of Oregon

Library of Congress Control Number: 2014908511

ISBN 13: 978-0-9886140-5-5
ISBN 10: 0988614057

First Printing 2014

10 9 8 7 6 5 4 3 2 1

Right: WillaKenzie Estate, page 210

Previous Page: Youngberg Hill Vineyards, page 242

 Panache Partners, LLC, is dedicated to the restoration and
conservation of the environment. Our books are manufactured
with strict adherence to an environmental management system in
accordance with ISO 14001 standards, including the use of paper
from mills certified to derive their products from well-managed forests.
We are committed to continued investigation of alternative paper
products and environmentally responsible manufacturing processes
to ensure the preservation of our fragile planet.

SPECTACULAR WINERIES
of Oregon

The sign on the post reads:

KNIGHT'S GAMBIT
VINEYARD

AN ERATH VINEYARDS
GRAPE GROWER

Food without wine is not meant to be. The connection between the two is a natural one. The correct pairing makes great wine greater, and cuisine exceptional. When you hit the pairing on the nose, sparks fly, emotions soar, and lasting memories are created. This relationship can provoke heated debates and rapturous discoveries, because everyone has their own ideas about what makes a good pairing.

I prefer to adopt my wife's directive for pairings, which is really no directive at all. And that is precisely why her "no rules, no guidelines" viewpoint has led us to many thrilling breakthroughs. Our life is a sum of our experiences, so why deny ourselves the sheer joy that wine and food is meant to bring?

We first discovered Oregon wines while living in New York City, even before we considered moving here. We tasted several young pinots: so vibrant, so full of vigor. The experience made us want more, made us wonder what this raw, untamed place called Oregon was all about. We longed to be a part of this bourgeoning last great frontier. One could say Oregon wine is the single most decisive reason why we live and work here today.

We saw the pioneering spirit that the winemaking men and women demonstrated. We wanted to share in this uniquely Oregon characteristic. The diverse grape-growing practices, developed through trial and error in this sometimes unpredictable climate and with these soils, makes it an exciting place to craft wine. The winemakers' commitment to, and understanding of, the importance of working with the rhythms of nature in an eco-friendly, sustainable manner have further served to put our region on the map. We believe that the movement in Oregon's food world to define the region's culinary identity is clearest in our vineyards.

With many splendid vintages behind us, we are able to explore and share so many more treasures our winemaking community has produced. Today our state has 17 approved AVAs, with more than 450 wineries growing 72 grape varieties. Hard to believe all this has happened since the day we moved here. To us, it means so many more opportunities for heated food and wine pairing debates and rapturous discoveries. To you, well, you just have to smell, swirl, sample, and sip your way through the wines in this book and maybe, just maybe, you will discover Oregon just as we did: a region full of life, vigor, and untamed possibilities.

Cheers and bon appétit,

Vitaly Paley

Chef; owner of Paley's Place Bistro and Bar,
Imperial, Portland Penny Diner; and co-author of
The Paley's Place Cookbook

Photograph by John Valls

Cherry Hill Winery, page 80

INTRODUCTION

The experts doubted the temperamental climate of Oregon; the verdant slopes seemed pretty enough, but wine industry leaders—from the professors at UC Davis to veterans of Napa Valley—were convinced that quality wine simply couldn't be produced in Oregon. But the climate was more like that of Burgundy, France, than just about any other place in the New World.

The early adventurous winemakers who ventured into the valleys of Oregon believed that the state's terroir was, in fact, the place for cool-climate wines like luxurious pinot noirs and crisp rieslings. Sure enough, pioneers like Charles Coury, Dick Erath, David Lett, and Richard Sommers planted parts of the state with these varietals and others, including pinot gris and chardonnay, to great success.

Brooks, page 54

Within a decade, other believers followed suit. Families with names that are synonymous with Oregon wine today—Adelsheim, Sokol Blosser, Vuylsteke—began putting down roots in the mid-1960s, where a nearly intact ecosystem greeted them with challenges unique to the virgin region.

A true labor of love, the early years of Oregon wine were not without trials, but every time a new wine pioneer embarked on his or her journey, the rest of the Oregon wine industry was there to help. This collaborative spirit exists to this day, and it is one of the characteristics that makes Oregon so unique. With shared advice, encouragement, and several laughs along the way, these pioneers brought the slopes of Oregon to world notice in the 1970s and 1980s, when Oregon pinot noirs began beating some of France's best labels at international competitions. It was clear that the experts had been wrong.

There's always talk of the soil in Oregon, and what winemakers and vineyard managers are doing to conserve it. Much of the land had been largely untouched before the first vineyards were planted, and the state's pioneers sought to keep the land as intact as possible. A culture of sustainable practices developed out of this love for the land.

When the Oregon Wine Board first began in the mid-1980s—albeit under a different name—its intent was to promote the marketing of Oregon wine while offering educational initiatives to help new winemakers hone their craft. The Board also began funding research projects with an eye toward supporting the industry's love of conservation.

Yamhill Valley Vineyards, page 236

Elk Cove Vineyards, page 110

Lemelson Vineyards, page 144

Maysara Winery, page 150

Kramer Vineyards, page 122

Penner-Ash Wine Cellars, page 170

To this day, the Oregon Wine Board strives to make sustainability possible through its partnerships with winery owners and the various certifying bodies in the state. One such organization, Low Input Viticulture and Enology, otherwise known as LIVE, was established by the state's vineyard owners specifically for the certification of sustainable growing practices for wine grapes. Its existence illustrates the dedication to the land that these wineries share.

Within this book you will read stories of former engineers who spend their second careers among the grapes with state-of-the-art, one-of-a-kind technology in the fermentation rooms. You will learn about vineyard owners who push the boundaries and accept when a new method works better in the production process. What you won't find, however, is a culture that uses innovative technologies just for technology's sake. Not men and women to follow trends, winemakers in Oregon change when

they need to, but keep a hands-off approach as their central goal, understanding that the best way to create exceptional wine is to create exceptional vines.

Like the diverse climates of the region, Oregon wineries are as varied as the vintages they produce. From large-scale facilities with cutting-edge technology unlike anything else in the wine world to charming family vineyards, you will find adventure and romance in the gently sloping hills and at the feet of Mount Hood and Mount Jefferson.

To prepare you for your journey, *Spectacular Wineries of Oregon* will take you on an eye-opening tour of the 17 American Viticultural Areas located within the state. Gorgeous photography and captivating descriptions make this landmark publication a wonderfully comprehensive guide to falling in love with Oregon wine.

CONTENTS

Apolloni Vineyards, page 32

OFF THE VINE

Willamette Valley Vineyards, page 216

Amalie Robert Estate, page 26

Archery Summit, page 34

Chehalem, page 74

Adelsheim Vineyard

Newberg

Adelsheim Vineyard was established during a different era in America, when an idealization of going back to the land, a vision of a lifestyle focused on wine, and faith in one's own abilities could stand in for a business plan.

In 1971, Ginny and David Adelsheim purchased the 19 acres that would become their Quarter Mile Lane Vineyard. They shared a dream with a handful of families that Oregon's climate and land could one day produce serious wines. A home was built, vines planted, and in 1978, the first commercial wines were produced.

As the Oregon wine industry has grown over the last five decades, Adelsheim Vineyard has grown along with it. In the course of that history, David became the vineyard manager, winemaker, and the person in charge of sales, marketing, accounting, and eventually, the person who hired smarter people to do all these jobs.

On behalf of the Oregon wine industry, he led work on clonal importation, wine labeling regulations, establishing statewide and regional industry organizations, and the creation of industry events, such as the International Pinot Noir Celebration and Oregon Pinot Camp. Today his principal role is strategic planning and extension of the Adelsheim brand.

The annual operation and long-term planning for all of the estate vineyards is overseen by the vineyard manager, Chad Vargas. The critical parts of the vineyard work are carried out by a 15-person vineyard crew, many of whom have been with the company for almost 30 years. Adelsheim's estate vineyards are all on hillsides and the sites have been sought out for their potential for growing the highest quality wine grapes. The historic focus of the estate has been in the Chehalem Mountains AVA, but Adelsheim has additional sites in Ribbon Ridge and the Eola-Amity Hills.

Top: Guests enjoy Adelsheim wine on the terrace at the winery in the summertime.

Bottom: David Adelsheim, co-founder and president of Adelsheim Vineyard.

Facing Page: Adelsheim's Bryan Creek Vineyard in the Chehalem Mountains AVA.
Photographs by Kent Derek Studio

The 10 Adelsheim estate vineyards are each very different. Some are big, some small, some at high elevations, some at lower elevations, some on volcanic soils, some on sedimentary soils, and their exposure varies from northeast to due west. Thus, there can be a huge variation in ripening times and in the flavors, tannins, sugars, and acidities of the grapes. To maximize grape quality so that Adelsheim finds new ways to make even better wines, Chad oversees a wide range of experiments in the estate vineyards each year.

Above: The tower at the entrance to the tasting room and winery.

Left: A view of the terrace in the springtime at the winery on Calkins Lane.
Photographs by Kent Derek Studio

Winemaker Dave Paige and his staff continue the experim   in the winery, keeping every lot separate so that the differences confer   y the experiments can be tracked and understood. Dave knows that ra   he bar with every growing season requires ceaseless attention to deta   m managing the crop size vine-by-vine to controlling 180 individual p   oir fermenters—all while staying focused on the big picture. His wine   am combines traditional and state-of-the-art techniques to produc   es that show elegance, complexity, balance, and richness in their   as, flavors, and textures.

At its core, Adelsheim Vineyard is about crafting wines in a style co   nt with their place. The objective in its estate vineyards is to refle   ch site and block as honestly as possible. It is only by understandir   ch individual block, by making small changes in management each   as their experience grows, that Adelsheim has been able to create th   ge of wines of superb quality for which it is known.

Ultimately it is the company's goal to be known as one of Oregon   at wine producers. The team will work to accomplish that by contir   to invest in great sites and talent, being leaders in their industry, collab   ng with their industry colleagues to find ways to market the region   ts wines to the world, and continuing to develop unique experiences   e winery for guests from around the US and the world.

Visitors to Adelsheim Vineyard always experience a premium wir   nt that showcases its exclusive single vineyard pinot noirs, available   at the winery or to club members. Tours provide an introduction to the   ns Lane Vineyard, a comprehensive overview of the winemaking facil   d a discussion of the winery's 40-plus year history in the Willamette

Top: Chad Vargas, viticulturist and vineyard manager; David Adelsheim, co-founder and pr Dave Paige, winemaker.

Middle: New vines being planted in block 23 at Calkins Lane Vineyard in spring 2010.

Bottom: The winery's barrel caves, where pinot noir and chardonnay are aged in French oa about 10 months.

Facing Page: Chardonnay, pinot blanc, pinot gris, and pinot noir are grown at Adelsheim's Creek Vineyard in the Chehalem Mountains AVA.
Photographs by Kent Derek Studio

WINE & FARE

Auxerrois, Ribbon Springs Vineyard, Ribbon Ridge
Enjoy with crab salad or cured salmon with tarragon dressing.

Caitlin's Reserve Chardonnay, Willamette Valley
Serve alongside poached salmon, lobster, smoked meats, and cheeses.

Elizabeth's Reserve Pinot Noir, Willamette Valley
Pairs beautifully with the pinot noir classics: lamb, duck, grilled salmon, and aged cheeses.

Quarter Mile Lane Vineyard Pinot Noir, Chehalem Mountains
Wonderful with grilled salmon, domestic and wild fowl, and other savory main dishes.

Tastings
Open to the public daily, year-round

Oregon has long been close to Mary Olson's heart. It was her 22-year career with a nati telecommunications company that landed the Wisconsin native in Oregon for two ye cultivating her love for the state and its wines. She told friends and family that in her "next she'd own a winery and live out her dream.

Turns out, Mary's dream was just within arm's reach. She took the plunge in 1997 purchased Airlie Winery, hired a winemaker, and packed up her office wardrobe in favo field-worthy attire. "I can remember that first harvest was one of Oregon's wettest, and were still smiling all the way through," says Mary of her drastic lifestyle change.

Established in 1986, Airlie is nestled in Oregon's coastal mountain range on the wes edge of the Willamette Valley and takes its name from a very small nearby town. The viney and the winery are LIVE certified sustainable. For Mary and winemaker Elizabeth Clark, philosophy hinges on the manner in which they treat the earth and their employees create wines that are sustainable for customers as well.

Elizabeth enjoys working with each of Airlie's varietals, which include chardonn gewürztraminer, maréchal foch, müller thurgau, pinot blanc, pinot gris, pinot noir, and riesl She's dedicated to unveiling each grape's distinctive characters, living up to her motto "serious whites and elegant reds," and continuing the dream at Airlie Winery.

Top: Pinot gris is Oregon's second-most widely planted grape after pinot noir and is known as Oregon's "other" pinot. Air is a beauty: crisp, dry, and refreshing.

Bottom: Owner Mary Olson and favorite passenger Riley cruise through the vineyard. Airlie is a dog-friendly winery offerin outdoor tastings, a picnic area, and a pond.

Facing Page: Winemaker Elizabeth Clark and Mary walk through Dunn Forest Vineyard, the 30-acre estate vineyard, in preparation for harvest.
Photographs by Andréa Johnson

Alloro Vineyard

Alloro Vineyard is 70 acres of uniquely contoured, loess-derived Laurelwood soil. Located on a southwest-facing slope descending from Laurel Ridge in the Chehalem Mountains, founder and vineyard manager David Nemarnik describes this special place as the heart and soul of Alloro. The name translates into Italian as laurel, the evergreen plant thought to symbolize immortality in ancient times. It was chosen by David as both a nod to his Italian-Croatian heritage and as a descriptive reference of the vineyard.

A fateful bicycle ride in the early 1990s led to David's discovery of this very special place. In 1999, Alloro's sustainably farmed vineyard was planted and soon became home to its Mediterranean-inspired, solar-powered winery and, ultimately, to a diverse mixture of many other crops, plants, and animals, establishing an extraordinary whole farm setting.

Educated at UC Davis, Burgundy-trained winemaker Tom Fitzpatrick was carefully chosen to craft Alloro's 100-percent estate, limited-production wines in a style that maintains the wine's inherent balance, captures its purity, liberates its hidden complexity, and displays its subtlety, elegance, and grace. Tom will tell you that a wine should be "an expression of place at a moment in time" and should therefore capture the unique personality of a site as it is expressed in each vintage. Terroir-driven wines that reflect this philosophy are what you'll find at Alloro. This inspiring connection of land and wine is a hallmark of the Alloro experience.

Top: Winemaker Tom Fitzpatrick works closely with Alloro's founder and vineyard manager, David Nemarnik.

Middle: Summer evenings are especially lovely on the tasting room patio.

Bottom: Alloro's estate pinot noir is award-winning.

Facing Page: Estate vineyards surround the winery and tasting room, where guests enjoy the "Whole Farm Dinner" every September.
Photographs by Andréa Johnson

Amalie Robert Estate

Dallas

Dena Drews and Ernie Pink founded Amalie Robert Estate on a simple idea: Make the best wine on the planet. No big deal, right? As it turns out, their past in the high-tech world would give them the necessary traits to make that happen. The key to winemaking, like technology, is to understand the fundamentals—in this case, estate-grown vines—and apply disciplined experiments. For Amalie Robert Estate, every year is a response to Mother Nature and an opportunity to experiment and learn. The vineyard is 30 acres of sustainably farmed vines located in the sedimentary foothills of the North Willamette Valley. Ernie found it hiding under an old cherry orchard. Pinot noir is ideally suited to this site and microclimate, but they also find great success with chardonnay, pinot meunier, syrah, and viognier. "You take what Mother Nature gives you," says Ernie, and your role is to steward the beauty and elegance of the vintage through to the bottle. In Oregon, every vintage is different and provides co-owners and co-winemakers Dena and Ernie an opportunity to express their hallowed ground with the "Hers and His" reserve pinot noirs. Hers is Amalie's Cuvée and his is Estate Selection.

"All roads lead to pinot noir," says Ernie. When you open a bottle of Amalie Robert Estate pinot noir, you taste the site; there's purity in each bottle that comes from care taken in the vineyard, stewardship in the winery, and blending estate-grown pinot noir for complexity, balance, and great intrigue. Crafting a well-educated palate is seriously fun business at Amalie Robert Estate. Come for a visit, and let Dena and Ernie give you that experience— through the vineyards with him, through the bottle with her. And that's the magic: Two people set out to discover what they were capable of, and what they are capable of is extraordinary. Wines true to the soil, wines true to the vintage.

Top: Dena Drews and Ernie Pink are the winery's co-founders and co-owners. Their respective middle names, Amalie and Robert, are the origin of Amalie Robert Estate.

Middle: Amalie Robert Estate was founded at the turn of the century. All of its wines are estate-grown and sustainably farmed.

Bottom: The pinot noir clusters slowly develop aromas and flavors just days before harvest.

Facing Page: The fermentation deck and twin-drive, dilithium chambers have a commanding presence.
Photographs by Andréa Johnson

Anderson Family Vineyard

Dundee Hills

When couriers trek up the quiet hillside in the Willamette Valley to Anderson Family Vineyard, they stop and stare for a moment. Hidden away like Oregon's very own wine gem, the vineyard—owned by Cliff and Allison Anderson—boasts views of the valley that command attention; views that unbiased visitors claim are the best in the region. Most people visit based on the word-of-mouth recommendations of friends or family, and the resulting experience is personal and casual, with candid conversations with the owners and winemaker while sampling a flight of wines. Those wines come from Anderson's unique, rocky soil. An old landslide location, the 20-acre hillside is essentially a pile of rocks, giving the grapes great drainage. Its hidden location adds a certain rustic charm to the vineyard: Located in the middle of Oregon's finest vineyards and wineries, a visit to Anderson opens up to views of Chehalem Ridge, the Dundee Hills, and two snow-capped peaks.

Like many winemakers, Cliff cites his family's farming legacy as inspiration. In a time before organic farming became popular, Cliff's grandfather was farming his land organically without the aid of pesticides. Today Cliff and Allison farm their vineyard using the same techniques, while enjoying the irony—Cliff's grandfather was a devout Prohibitionist.

Cliff and Allison purchased their vineyard in 1989, then cleared and planted it with chardonnay, pinot noir, and pinot gris grapes in 1992. Initially a commercial grape supplier for area wineries, Anderson Family Vineyard began producing estate wines in 2002. The winemaking process at the winery is, according to Cliff, "sanely scientific." The Andersons—who have been making wine since they were too young to drink it—apply low-tech, hands-on techniques that allow the beauty of the grapes to blossom into the wine.

Top: Allison and Cliff Anderson are the founders, farmers, and winemakers.

Bottom: The French oak barrel of pinot noir has a bubbler to off-gas carbon dioxide from the secondary fermentation.

Facing Page: The view is breathtaking as the sun rises over Chehalem Ridge, just above The Allison Inn & Spa. The rock walls are courtesy of the Andersons' Irish son-in-law, Chris Robinson.
Photographs by Andréa Johnson

Described as big, bold, bottled sunshine, the pinot noir is highly structured, with a deep backbone of complex fruit. It possesses a spicy potpourri of Asian five spice: cinnamon and ginger, backed by plum and black cherry flavors. With an intriguing aroma that can only be described as marine air, evoking the smells of fresh ocean air, it is intensely flavorful. The pinot noir unfolds in layers, and like the vineyard itself, reveals hidden gems throughout the experience.

The beautifully aged chardonnay is mineral-rich, full of spice, and boasts a luxurious mouthfeel. Having minimal oak influence, Anderson Family chardonnay boasts flavors of ripe pear and pie spice that mingle with a creamy yet bright citrus flavor—a true gem.

Above: Wine barrels rest deep in the subterranean cave. Tasting finished barrels and listening to the active ones are highlights of touring the barrel cellar.

Left: Classic Oregon pinot noir lights up the wine glass. Specializing in Burgundian varietals, the Andersons also grow Dijon chardonnay and a tiny amount of pinot gris.

Facing Page: Anderson Family Vineyard is all Oregon. Rustic barn buildings belong, as do the array of native plantings around the winery.
Photographs by Andréa Johnson

WINE & FARE

Anderson Family Vineyard Pinot Noir
Serve alongside slow-roasted salmon or pistachio-crusted venison loin.

Anderson Family Vineyard Chardonnay
Pairs well with Dungeness crab or game bird ravioli.

Anderson Family Vineyard Pinot Gris
Elegant alongside curried squash bisque or ripe Alsatian Munster-géromé.

Tastings
Open by appointment only

Apolloni Vineyards

Forest Grove

Many wineries begin with a break from the ordinary. For others, it is the unfolding of a longstanding tradition. Apolloni Vineyards is most certainly one of the latter. The Apolloni family traces its winemaking roots to the Arezzo region in Tuscany, Italy, more than 150 years ago. Alfredo Apolloni, a first-generation American who grew up on the family winery in Italy, reinvigorates that history in the Willamette Valley, focusing on the three fundamental principles of tradition, Italian heritage, and family. As owner and head winemaker, Alfredo ensures that each bottle from Apolloni Vineyards brings with it a blending of the Old World and the new.

Alfredo and his wife, Laurine, bought 62 acres in 1999, and have since added another 40. With pinot noir being something akin to the hometown juice, the Apollonis focus on this varietal, with a number of whites and a few Italian varietals for good measure. The family keeps the winery's operation in the hands of the few, preferring to touch every bottle for quality assurance. The wines go through small-lot fermentation and spend an almost unheard-of 16 to 18 months in barrels in order to create a more pleasant taste in the glass. Using sustainable agriculture, avoiding all fertilizer—they even dry-farm as natural water sources supply their needs—the Apolloni team runs a tight winemaking process, relatively unchanged for centuries. Great fruit is the heart of great wine, and you'll find both in each bottle from Apolloni Vineyards.

Top: Of Italian heritage, owner-winemaker Alfredo Apolloni carefully crafts wines that nod to his past while showing a deep sense of the present.

Middle: The adventures of grape growing and winemaking are cherished traditions of the Apollinis: Adolfo, Giulia, Laura, Laurine, and Alfredo.

Bottom: Work and play are both important to the Apolloni lifestyle. The family enjoys spending time at the winery bocce courts.

Facing Page: Nestled in the foothills of the Coastal Range, the sustainably farmed estate vineyards produce chardonnay, pinot blanc, pinot gris, pinot noir, and sangiovese.
Photographs by Andréa Johnson

Archery Summit

Dayton

The direct connection between the land and the wine is overwhelmingly apparent, and at Archery Summit, this principle guides the entire winemaking process. Specializing in pinot noir, the winemaking team headed by Christopher Mazepink, takes on the seamless process of melding the qualities of the land and the skill of the hand to craft Archery Summit wines. Since its founding in 1993, the team at Archery Summit has taken advantage of the exceptional growing conditions of the Willamette Valley to produce luxurious pinot noir and distinctive pinot gris. More than 120 planted acres span six estate vineyards: Arcus Estate, Archer's Edge Estate, Archery Summit Estate, Red Hills Estate, and Renegade Ridge Estate are in the Dundee Hills AVA, and Looney Vineyard is in the Ribbon Ridge AVA. One hundred percent of the grapes that go into Archery Summit wines come from these vineyards, ensuring that the team has complete control over every step of the process.

The sustainably farmed properties, some organic and some biodynamic, yield pinot noir and a small amount of pinot gris grapes at Archery Summit. The vines are planted in a traditional Burgundian spacing with up to 4,800 plants per acre of land. This method forces each vine to carry a smaller amount of fruit that is higher in concentration and flavor. The grapes are then hand-harvested, ensuring the preservation of the delicate fruit. Non-interventionist in method, Christopher lets the wines develop on their own, including about eight percent of the grapes to be fermented as whole clusters to give the wines additional spice and complexity. The grapes are fermented in a combination of both wooden and stainless steel tanks in the five-level winery that is exclusively gravity-flow. This gentle handling is critical to preserving all the natural flavors that the grape has to offer. The wine is then stored in a natural underground cave where temperatures are maintained at a constant 55 degrees year-round.

Top: Christopher Mazepink is the general manager and winemaker.
Photograph by Richard Knapp

Bottom: Archery Summit Premier Cuvée Pinot Noir is a blend comprised of fruit from the winery's six estate vineyards in the Dundee Hills and Ribbon Ridge appellations.
Photograph by Richard Knapp

Facing Page: Arcus Estate is a dramatic expanse of vineyard blocks that have been procured by Archery Summit over time. Arcus, which means "bow" in Latin, is aptly named for its steep, bowl-shaped configuration.
Photograph by Andréa Johnson

In a region dominated by pinot noir, Archery Summit is home not only to the Willamette Valley's prized varietal, but also a unique pinot gris, epitomized in its Ab Ovo bottling. Capitalizing on the fact that pinot berries respond to variances in methodologies, Ab Ovo Pinot Gris is fermented in an egg-shaped concrete fermentor—the wine's name means "from the egg." The concrete adds a unique minerality to the limited production wine, which now boasts a cult following.

From Archery Summit's six estate vineyards, single-vineyard pinot noirs continue to thrill the palates of wine drinkers. The Arcus Estate Pinot Noir reveals aromas of blueberry cobbler, dark plum, and luscious black cherries. Flavors of marionberry, cinnamon stick, and black huckleberry earned the 2010 bottling 93 points from *The Wine Advocate*.

Above: Archery Summit was deliberately built as a gravity-fed winery, with the purpose of transferring the wine from tank to barrel as gently and naturally as possible.

Right: Christopher tastes Ab Ovo Pinot Gris from its unique concrete fermentation vessel.

Facing Page Top: Pinot noir grapes are hand-harvested on a fall morning in the Dundee Hills.

Facing Page Bottom: During fermentation, the grape skins are punched down by hand up to three times per day to maximize extraction of flavor and color.
Photographs by Andréa Johnson

Both novices and connoisseurs love the Premier Cuvée Pinot Noir, with its elegant floral and spice aromas. Its expansive palate displays notes of ripe cherries, blackberries, and anise with hints of cinnamon stick. Ripe tannins have a velvety quality that gives way to a clean, lingering finish. Wines produced by Archery Summit are consistently lauded by Robert Parker's *The Wine Advocate* and *Wine Spectator* magazine as among the best bottlings in the world. In 2009, First Lady Michelle Obama served the 2004 Archery Summit Estate Pinot Noir at the first White House state dinner during her husband's presidency. Paired alongside wagyu beef and Nantucket scallops with glazed red carrots, the wine made its Capitol Hill debut in style. Guests to the winery have the opportunity to sample these and other wines, some directly from the barrel depending upon tour availability. Food and wine pairings allow visitors to sample the luxurious wines alongside distinctive cuisine choices, and a variety of events are scheduled throughout the year.

Above: Guests gather during the Symphony in the Vineyard summer event, an elegant evening of wine, food, and music at Arcus Estate with the Portland Symphony.

Left: Guests enjoy the winery's lively annual Crab Feast dinner held in the fermentation hall.

Facing Page: Archery Summit was the first winery in Oregon to bore an extensive set of underground caves, modeled after those in Burgundy's Côte d'Or, in which to store maturing wine in-barrel.
Photographs by Andréa Johnson

Premier Cuvée Pinot Noir
Pairs elegantly with roast duck and mushrooms in a light wine sauce.

Vireton Pinot Gris
Serve alongside grilled shrimp and fresh herb risotto.

Archery Summit Estate Pinot Noir
Pairs well with grilled leg of lamb, marinated in garlic confit with fresh thyme.

Ab Ovo Pinot Gris
Pair with rich crab cakes and sautéed asparagus.

Tastings
Open to the public daily

August Cellars

Newberg

When German emigrant August Schaad made a new home with his wife, Anna, on Parrett Mountain, he set in motion a family legacy that would last for generations. It was 1903 and the couple established a family farm, raising seven children. Their eldest, Clarence Schaad, purchased 42 acres of farmland in 1942 that now serves as the home for August Cellars—a winery dedicated to creating delicious and affordable wine, all while keeping the family farm intact. Clarence's two surviving children, Lewis and Grace, both retired schoolteachers, carried on the family tradition once again. Lewis' two sons, Tom and Jim, operate August Cellars, which opened for business in 2002.

Named after August Schaad, August Cellars is the modern-day equivalent to a new farming venture. The youngest of his generation, Tom credits the winery's success to the fact that the entire family recognizes and respects each other's role within the company. For example, while Tom manages the facility his brother, Jim, tends to the winemaking, and their aunt works in the tasting room.

The trend of working together continues further, as August Cellars is also a host for seven other wineries. The collaborative arrangement was an important deciding factor in the location and type of building the Schaads chose for August Cellars. The winery is on the steep and narrow part of the farm, which was not conducive to traditional farming, and above it are the orchards. Now it's inhabited by 25 acres of mature English walnut trees, nine acres of Italian prunes, a 13-acre pinot noir plot—leased to another winery—and six acres of wooded area. The 16,000-square-foot winery facility is located at the bottom of the orchards, near Highway 99 West. The winery's barrel rooms are tucked deep into the hillside there.

Top: Maréchal Foch is one of the bigger, more rustic wines produced by August Cellars.

Bottom: Tom Schaad takes a quick break on the front patio before harvest starts for the day.

Facing Page: The walnut orchard is bracketed between the wind turbine and the winery. The vineyard, timber, and back orchard behind the turbine complete the family farm.
Photographs by Andréa Johnson

The total production at the winery is about 8,000 cases, 2,000 of which are produced by August Cellars, so a large storage space as well as the ability to bottle all wine in-house was important to the Schaads. They feel it produces a collaborative spirit, setting them apart from other well-rehearsed wine regions like California or France. "In Oregon, we're all small and we all know we have to work together to be really successful," says Tom. "Being a winery that is also a host winery really captures that image and that spirit." August Cellars purchases all the fruit for its own wines then processes and bottles them on-site in its facility. These include cabernet sauvignon, maréchal foch, merlot, pinot noir—a dark rustic red—baco noir, chardonnay, gewürztraminer, pinot gris, riesling, and rosé. Though they have a very popular pinot noir, Tom and Jim look to focus on more than just a single varietal. After all, their mission is to create a full brand of tasteful and affordable wines; bottles range from only $12 to $30. The brothers say these are the best kind of wines—the ones to be shared over dinner with family and friends.

Top: Three generations still come together to harvest walnuts. Grace, Tom, Lewis, and Matt lead by example, showing how to pick English walnuts.

Bottom: Tasting room manager Charles Garrell walks past the barrel rooms, bringing another case of wine to the tasting room.

Facing Page: Tom looks on as Jim punches down pinot noir, with Chris Dickson of Ribera Vineyard on the second floor doing the same. Fermentors are tarped to keep fruit flies out.
Photographs by Andréa Johnson

Chardonnay
Serve with white sauces and cheese dishes, such as clam chowder or fettuccini alfredo.

Riesling
A classic German pairing includes brats fresh off the grill, slathered in great mustard, or a pizza.

Pinot Noir
Pairs well with grilled tuna, salmon, and dry-rubbed pork chops.

Maréchal Foch
Pair with big flavorful foods, wild mushrooms, lamb kabobs, and steak.

Tastings
Open to the public daily May through October and weekends only November through April

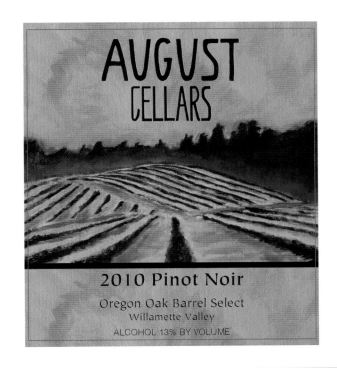

BelleFiore Winery Estate & Vineyard

Ashland

The magnificence of blending art and science defines BelleFiore Winery Estate & Vineyard. At first glance, the Italian-style wine pavilion invites inspiration and curiosity. Looking above the elegant vineyards, eyes are fixed upon the graceful, French-inspired château. The name BelleFiore is a blend of French and Italian, and you can see the team's fascination with those cultures throughout the winery. The fusion of European cultures and the sciences of enology and viticulture are cherished at BelleFiore.

Three themes—art, science, and education—dominate every step along the path to embrace the art of winemaking. Founder Edward Kerwin and the creative operations team at BelleFiore bring to bear classical art, architecture, and the science of winemaking. Once a specialist in solar energy alternatives for NASA, now a scientific researcher and immunologist, Dr. Kerwin has a deep passion for art and science, which inspires BelleFiore's team of talented, committed managers and staff. The winery features nine miles of underground geothermal heating and cooling pipes, a naturally efficient and constant energy source that provides sustainable heating and cooling throughout the tank rooms, barrel rooms, and visitor areas.

Planted in 2006, the original 35 acres now boast 15 varietals, including Bordeaux and Burgundy grapes and rarities like Montepulciano and coda di volpe. The hand-picked clusters and hand-sorted grapes are processed on state-of-the-art equipment with laboratory-level cleanliness. The whole process is extraordinarily energy efficient; there is nothing like BelleFiore in the region. Award-winning wines, including celebrated pinot noirs, delectable Bordeaux "Numinos" blends, and mysterious Montepulciano, Teroldego, and coda di volpe intrigue the palate.

Top: Located in the Bear Creek, Rogue Valley AVA, the winery welcomes visitors year-round to its 35,000-square-foot wine pavilion.

Middle: Producing a remarkable variety of wines, BelleFiore is committed to empowering customers and enriching their experiences.

Bottom: Touring BelleFiore is often described as a transcendental experience, and the estate's rich architecture alone would be worth the visit. The Numinos banquet room features a wall of windows looking out to the breathtaking vineyards.

Facing Page: The French-inspired château recalls the Old World.
Photographs by April Metternich, All Rights Reserved, BelleFiore Winery

Benton-Lane Winery

Monroe

Wine is a true, lifelong passion for Benton-Lane Winery founders Carol and Steve Girard. One of Carol's earliest memories was, as a little girl, accompanying her father downstairs into her family's wine cellar to select the evening's bottle. Her father's experience in World War II Europe as a young man left him with a devoted passion for wine. Steve's father also spent a large amount of time in Europe and became enamored with wine, passing that passion to his son. Unsurprisingly, the couple began collecting wine as soon as they were married. The high school sweethearts also found themselves living in Napa Valley a few years after tying the knot. There, they worked alongside some of Napa's great winemakers, growing grapes, making fine wine, and learning the ropes of the wine industry.

The couple's first winery, Girard Winery, was founded in the Oakville Bench in the heart of Napa Valley. Carol and Steve were very involved in the Napa wine industry. Steve was elected to both the board of the Napa Valley Vintners' Association and The Wine Institute Board of Directors. Girard wines graced tables at White House state dinners, and Julia Child selected the winery for an event that involved pairing Girard wines with her famous dishes. But as time evolved, so did their tastes. Cooking lighter, fresher, and healthier cuisine in their home kitchen, the couple found that they wanted to pair the dishes with elegant Burgundy-style pinot noir. They considered planting a vineyard they already owned on a Yountville hillside with pinot noir grapes, but recognized that the region was still too warm for the cooler climate varietal. So they began looking northward for a suitable location.

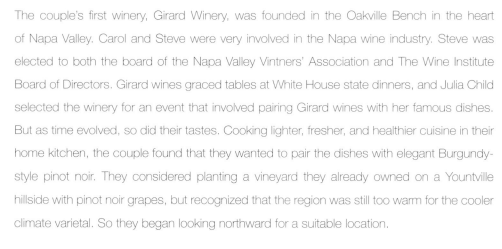

Top: Displaying the long history and journey of Carol and Steve Girard's passion for wine are three estate-grown wines: Reserve Cabernet Sauvignon—from their Oakville Bench vineyards and Yountville hillside vineyards in Napa Valley—alongside first-class pinot noir and chardonnay from the Willamette Valley.

Bottom: Focused on making the finest wines for more than three decades, Steve and Carol are proud of their barrel room.

Facing Page: Benton-Lane's 147-acre planted estate vineyards are surrounded by more than 600 acres of natural riparian habitat.
Photographs by Robert Holmes

Their years-long search took them to Oregon, just south of Portland, but the established vineyard sites they toured just didn't seem quite right. Then Steve discovered a jewel in SunnyMount Ranch, a sheep ranch that had been in operation for a century. The soils were rich in organic material and untouched by chemicals. An added bonus was denoted in the ranch's name. The location is protected by Prairie Peak to the west and receives more sunlight than the surrounding areas. Senior pilots in the area have long referred to the location as the "keyhole" because it is the one cloudless location on a descent into consistently overcast Eugene and Corvallis, Oregon.

Stretching over 145 acres of prime vineyard, Benton-Lane Winery is planted with several clones and rootstocks. Steve established the vineyards as non-irrigated. This forces the grapevines to push deep into the soils to find new nutrients, creating a strong vine and flavorful grapes. Organic materials from the winemaking process, such as grape skins, seeds, and stems, go back into the soils along with fresh organics, rock flour, mint plants, and corn silage at the perfect pH to replenish any nutrients removed by the vines at a tenfold rate. A true reflection of place, even the winery's name expresses the location, which straddles Benton and Lane counties.

Above: Steve and Carol, circa 1980, stand beside their Girard Winery in Oakville, Napa Valley.
Photograph courtesy of Benton-Lane Winery

Left: The owners enjoy pouring at the tasting bar in Benton-Lane's on-site tasting room.
Photograph by Robert Holmes

Much like the pinot noir grape itself, Benton-Lane Winery is a harmonious blend of the Old World with the new. A lyrical space, both aesthetic and functional, the winery features a picturesque patio overlooking the Willamette Valley and Mount Jefferson. The patio is surrounded by organic herbs, vegetables, and flowers that are used in the couple's kitchen. Although the winery's reputation has been built on its exquisite pinot noirs, Benton-Lane has received many accolades for its other varietals, including four Top 100 Wines of the World awards. History has a way of repeating itself, as does the family's excellence that began in Napa. For his winemaking passion and dedication to being a good steward of the land, Steve was appointed by the governor of Oregon as a founding board member of the Oregon Wine Board. The winery's continued dedication to excellence at affordable prices makes the family-owned, estate-grown winery a favorite of novices and connoisseurs alike.

Above: Blair Girard, Carol and Steve's daughter, greets guests at a wine club event on the picturesque patio overlooking the Willamette Valley and snowcapped Mount Jefferson.
Photograph courtesy of Benton-Lane

Left & Facing Page: Benton-Lane has a wonderful barrel room where Steve enjoys sampling.
Photograph by Robert Holmes

WINE & FARE

Benton-Lane Pinot Noir
Delicious with salmon and all pasta dishes.

Benton-Lane Pinot Gris
Excellent with British Columbia shellfish and Asian-influenced dishes.

Benton-Lane Chardonnay
Perfect alongside lobster, risotto, and poultry dishes.

Tastings
Open to the public, seasonally

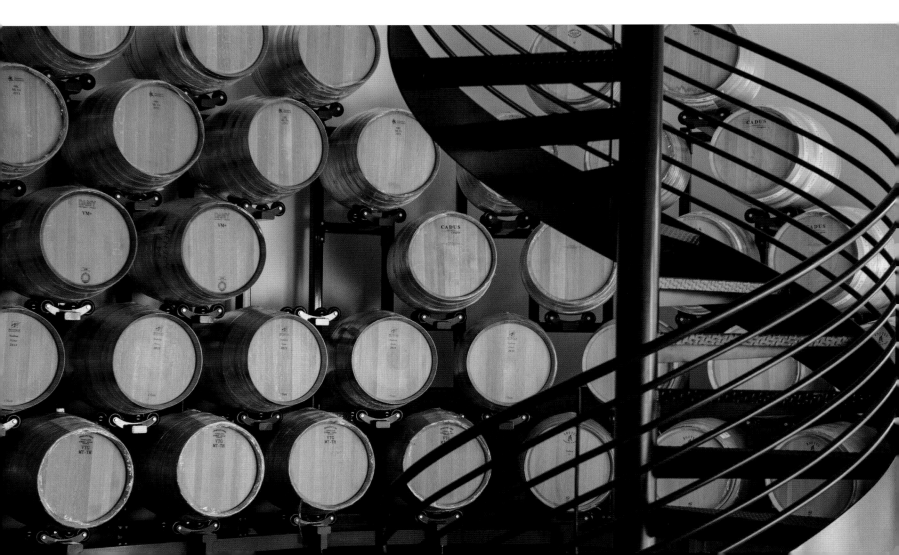

A Blooming Hill
Vineyard & Winery

Cornelius

As guests round the corner to A Blooming Hill Vineyard & Winery, Gemini and Trouble, fondly known as the property's "wine dogs," greet them. The tail-wagging pooches proudly lead the way past Jim and Holly Witte's blossoming vineyard to the tasting room. It's truly a home-based operation, as the couple lives on the property. Part of their abode even serves as the quaint, cozy tasting room, and the outdoor patio and teahouse is where they tied the knot in 2006. Visitors always remark that they feel like friends or invited guests.

The apple didn't far fall from the tree: Jim's love of farming stems from his grandfather, a Midwestern fruit farmer who also made his own fruit wine. In 2000, Jim purchased land and planted vineyards every two years through 2008, resulting in chardonnay, pinot gris, pinot noir, and riesling. A fourth block of grüner veltliner is in the planning stage.

Touting breathtaking panoramas of Mount Hood, A Blooming Hill—which produces an average of 800 to 1,200 cases of wine per year—occupies a southeastern-facing slope of windblown, rich volcanic soil. Surrounding elevation protects the vines from harsh climates, and Jim tends to each one by hand, beginning with the season's first pruning in January. He selects only the best clusters of fully formed grapes for fermentation.

In the fall of 2013, the Wittes debuted Jim's pinot-style port wine. It's no surprise they've capitalized so well on the varietal; their 2011 variety won a double gold from the Oregon Wine Awards and their 2010—one of Jim's all-time favorites—earned three silver medals. "Someone in the tasting room said to me, 'You can taste the winemaker's handwriting in all the wine,'" says Holly. "It's Jim's handwriting that we're known for."

Top: The oldest pinot noir vines are adjacent to the winery and outbuildings.

Middle: A doctor's piano buggy on the path to the tasting room makes a fun prop for photographs of wedding parties and kids alike.

Bottom: The tasting room patio is the perfect place for a picnic.

Facing page: A glance eastward reveals the oldest pinot noir vines and, in the distance, the newest blocks as well.
Photographs by Andréa Johnson

Sometimes, all it takes is one good bottle of wine to set you off on an unexpected career path. This was the case with Jimi Brooks, the founder of Brooks winery in Amity, Oregon. After graduating from college, Jimi left for Europe, finding work in the heart of France's Beaujolais region. He discovered the impact a specific site can have on the vines if the winemaker approaches his craft with a goal of transparency. Exposure to the pinot noir planted in nearby Burgundy solidified his thinking, but it was a bottle of Alsatian riesling that spoke loudest to Jimi: Its ability to translate the essence of place into a glass of wine was deeply inspiring. He had found his calling.

Upon returning to Oregon, Jimi continued to gain practical experience by working for other estates and wineries until 1998, when 300 cases of wine were produced under his own Brooks label. These first releases—the Janus Pinot Noir and Willamette Valley Riesling— established the philosophies of farming and winemaking that remain to this day the heart and soul behind every bottle produced by Brooks.

Brooks adheres to biodynamic farming principles. Biodynamics is the belief that all aspects of the vineyard—the soil, the weather, the insects, the community—are interconnected, and that respect for each element elevates the health of the vines and the quality of the grapes. Estate-produced compost replaces industrial sprays, vineyard work is scheduled with an awareness of astrological impact, and vineyard management decisions maximize the biodiversity of the entire property. "If the vine is happy, the grapes simply taste better," Jimi once said. "I believe that farming in this way, by keeping the earth alive and the ecosystem intact, is the only way to truly demonstrate the concept of terroir in wine."

Top: Riesling vines in the Brooks Estate Vineyard were planted in 1975, making them among the oldest of that variety planted in Oregon.
Photograph by Andréa Johnson

Bottom: Winery founder Jimi Brooks.
Photograph courtesy of Brooks

Facing Page: Brooks' Estate Vineyard. The original blocks of pinot noir and riesling were planted between 1973 and 1977 and are still on their own rootstock. In 2012, the biodynamic vineyard practices used by Brooks were certified by Demeter, the international organization that establishes these most stringent of farming standards.
Photograph by Andréa Johnson

When you taste a wine from Brooks, you taste that wine's vineyard origins as much as you do its winemaking technique. This is because the wine is never forced. Over time, growers learn what works best in their vineyard and cultivate their vines accordingly. Located in the heart of the Willamette Valley's Eola Hills, Brooks found riesling—so often an overlooked variety in the US—to be an extremely versatile and aromatic wine that captures the essence of the site while retaining its superb varietal character. As is the case with the Brooks pinot noir, Brooks riesling is an exciting statement on the endless possibilities that Oregon wine and Oregon soil can offer. Farmed naturally and made with a minimally invasive winemaking approach, the Brooks catalog is a challenge to other winemakers everywhere, daring them to reach for purity.

Take the Ara Riesling, a wine that found its way onto the table during a White House state dinner. The wine is made from the best riesling the Brooks Estate Vineyard offers and shows a dazzling power that, like its namesake constellation, brightens the corner of the universe it sits in. Here you'll find citrus, jasmine, and honeysuckle; a full-bodied experience tied together with tinges of herbs. The Rastaban Pinot Noir, a favorite of consumers and critics alike, is one of Brooks' rare single-vineyard bottles, made entirely from grapes grown in the Brooks Estate Vineyard. Although Jimi held a strong belief that blending wine from several vineyards produced wines of great depth, flavor, and balance, Rastaban showcases what happens when you use only the best barrels from the estate. It captures the place, it captures the excitement, and it captures the heart.

Left: Pascal Brooks, Janie Brooks Heuck, and Chris Williams in the Brooks Estate Vineyard.
Photograph by Andréa Johnson

Life, like a vineyard, has a cycle. In 2004, Jimi passed away at 38, leaving his son Pascal, who was 8 years old at the time, as sole owner of Brooks. The shock of Jimi's passing soon turned into his legacy. Winemaker friends who had gathered at his memorial compelled the family to carry on the winery and Jimi's philosophy. A dozen of Oregon's top winemakers saw the 2004 vintage through to bottling, and in 2005, Chris Williams, who was Jimi's assistant, became head winemaker. And Jimi's sister, Janie Brooks Heuck, took over the role of managing director, completing the circle of Brooks' core values of friendship, family, and spirit.

Above: The vertically designed, green facility centralizes all aspects of winemaking, sales, and hospitality.
Rendering courtesy of Brooks

Left: The Brooks Willamette Valley Riesling is a blend from the winery's top vineyards. Aged in stainless steel vessels to maintain freshness, the wine has additional time to evolve in the bottle before release.
Photograph by Andréa Johnson

Facing Page: Pascal Brooks, Janie Brooks Heuck, and Chris Williams with one of the riesling tanks. Chris describes harvest: "Once the grapes start coming in, it's an everyday, day-in and day-out kind of a job that you have to put everything you have into, right until you've got nothing left. Hopefully by that point, harvest is over."
Photograph by Andréa Johnson

Wine on its own is not magical—it's best consumed with good friends and good food to fully appreciate its ability to inspire the mind and heart. Brooks wines speak an old language, delivering an Oregonian experience filtered through a European sensibility. Discover the subtle impact of a sense of place, inspired by family and community.

Above: A Willamette Valley sunset over the Brooks vineyard. The Willamette Valley lies on the 45th parallel, halfway between the North Pole and the Equator, giving the vines long hours of sunlight each day and significant diurnal temperature swings between day and night. Grapevines thrive under these conditions, resulting in complex wines.
Photograph by Andréa Johnson

Top Left: In addition to riesling and pinot noir, Brooks produces wine made from gewürztraminer, pinot blanc, pinot gris, and a rosé.
Photograph by Clay McLachlan

Bottom Left: The grape cap—grape skins, seeds, and pulp—is pressed down into the juice to intensify flavor, aromatics, and color in Brooks Pinot Noir.
Photograph by Andréa Johnson

Facing Page Top: The Brooks logo represents the circle of life. Jimi wore this design as a tattoo long before it became a symbol of the winery. The image depicts the Ouroboros, a Greek term for a tail-devouring dragon that signifies infinity and unity. Also known as a representation of reincarnation, it inspires hope that a significant life cannot be extinguished.
Logo courtesy of Brooks

Facing Page Bottom: In autumn, the leaves turn golden amber after harvest. Over the winter each vine will be pruned and the vineyard's cycle of life will begin again.
Photograph by Andréa Johnson

Brooks Rastaban Pinot Noir
(100% biodynamically farmed pinot noir from the Brooks Estate Vineyard)
Serve with duck, pork, lamb, or a selection of artisanal cheeses.

Brooks Ara Riesling
*(Sustainably and biodynamically farmed grapes
from the Brooks Estate Vineyard and Yamhill Vineyards)*
Pair with seafood, poultry, or fresh vegetarian dishes.

Brooks Janus Pinot Noir
*(Blended from sustainably and biodynamically farmed grapes
from the Brooks Estate and five other nearby vineyards)*
Pair with pork, grilled chicken, or mushrooms.

Tastings
Open to the public Tuesday through Sunday,
by appointment only on Monday

B R O O K S

Carabella Vineyard
Wilsonville

The vision for Carabella Vineyard began when a fishing trip in Oregon sidetracked into wine tasting with some of Oregon's pioneer winemakers. Soon thereafter, Colorado geologist Mike Hallock began a 12-year journey to seek out an exceptional site for pinot noir in Oregon. In addition to his geology career in Denver, he became a cellar rat at a winery in downtown Denver—really!—took winemaking classes at UC Davis, and met his wife-to-be, Cara. Wondering why his "geology" office was covered with soils maps of Oregon, she urged him to dial the number on a two-line real estate ad. This led to a lasting friendship with the McDonald family and the purchase of the southeast-facing Ladd Hill site on Parrett Mountain.

The former Christmas tree farm was planted by viticulturist Mark Benoit and Mike Hallock in the spring of 1996. Volcanic soils, including Saum, Nekia, and Jory, provided excellent drainage, allowing dry farming. Dry-farming techniques embrace the variability of weather to fully express the mystique of vintage variation. The vineyard has 59 planted acres, all grafted vines: it also includes 13 blocks of pinot noir—Pommard, Wädenswil, and five Dijon clones—two blocks of Dijon 76 chardonnay, and two different clonal blocks of pinot gris. Farming is LIVE certified sustainable, featuring the ongoing re-establishment of native cover crops. The top of the vineyard, with an elevation of 600 feet, offers a magnificent view of five snow-covered volcanoes, with Mount Hood looming directly east.

The first crush was in 1998, with Cara holding down the Colorado life while Mike commuted to Oregon for harvest. In the fall of 2002, the family drove the modern-day covered wagon from Colorado to Oregon to pursue the Oregon pinot noir dream. They found a house near the vineyard and began living the country life in earnest, complete with daughter Eve's champion 4-H roosters.

Top: Mike, Cara, and Eve Hallock are Carabella Vineyard's proprietors.

Bottom: Inchinnan Pinot Noir is distinguished by depth, power, and black fruit.

Facing Page: Wildflowers are a lovely addition to the rows of grapes.
Photographs by Andréa Johnson

The Carabella winemaking philosophy is focused first on quality in the vineyard, as Mike makes all Carabella wines from 100-percent estate fruit. Sixty-five percent of Carabella is planted to pinot noir. Mike has been able to create distinctive pinot noir bottlings from the 13 blocks of pinot, foremost of which is the flagship Estate Blend. Each Carabella limited edition pinot noir has a distinctive signature. The power of Inchinnan, the elegance of Eve's Garden, or the happy accident of Mistake Block are departures from the Estate Blend.

A family trip to Burgundy's Meursault region has been the inspiration for the chardonnay style: barrel-fermented in French oak—only one-sixth new—with the remainder in neutral barrels to add layers of interest. Stony soil of the cooler north block of Dijon 76 features crisp minerality, while the east block contributes vivid fruit and aromatics to the cuvée. Carabella Estate Pinot Gris aspires to a fruit forward Oregon style with notes of pear and apricot. Both white wines feature lively acidity to better pair with seafood and poultry.

Above: A morning stroll between the pinot noir and chardonnay is one of life's simple pleasures.
Photograph by Andréa Johnson

Left: In December, the vines are dormant and the view of Mount Hood is majestic as always.
Photograph by Mike Hallock

Facing Page: Pommard gathers the morning's first light.
Photograph by Andréa Johnson

Inchinnan Pinot Noir
Pairs well with grilled lamb chops and a marionberry-chipotle glaze.

Mistake Block Pinot Noir
Elegant alongside pheasant pot pie.

Chardonnay Dijon 76 Estate
Serve with baked Oregon monkfish in a cream sauce with spring leeks.

Estate Pinot Gris
Perfect with freshly caught Dungeness crab.

Tastings
Open Thanksgiving and Memorial Day weekends and by appointment

Carabella

2011 | PINOT NOIR

CHEHALEM MOUNTAINS ▪ OREGON

ESTATE

Pinot Noir: 1997
Pommard X 3309C

Carabella

The Carlton Winemakers Studio

Carlton

Tucked into the charming wine village of Carlton, Oregon, The Carlton Winemakers Studio is surrounded by bucolic vineyards, orchards, and grass fields. It serves not only as a refuge for the visiting wine connoisseur, but also as home to an alternating selection of vintners who produce some of the region's most interesting varietals—all under one roof.

The bold brainchild of two couples, winemakers Eric Hamacher and Luisa Ponzi, and their partners, Kirsten and Ned Lumpkin of Lazy River Vineyard, the innovative studio was the first of its kind in Oregon when it launched in 2002. It was built on the foursome's vision of a place where boutique, independent labels could collectively share state-of-the-art equipment to craft premier vintages, while also maximizing sustainability and minimizing the ecological footprint of production. Armed with an exceptional cooperative spirit, the facility, which was built to LEED certification standards, acts as a wine incubator where newer winemakers can collaborate with veteran producers. The studio can host as many as 10 vintners, working side-by-side to create some of the region's best wines.

The unique positioning of The Carlton Winemakers Studio was well noted by Paul Gregutt of *The Seattle Times*, who described it as a "great one-stop opportunity to taste through some of the newest and rarest of the region's offerings, and a lesson in green engineering." Indeed, so diverse is the group of vintners housed onsite that a trip to the property's tasting room offers a broad, unparalleled snapshot of the Willamette Valley, with rich selections that range beyond the enticing pinot noir. "The winemaking is heartfelt. The wineries are small, independent and taking on the world," concluded *National Geographic Traveler* of this distinctive destination.

Top: The Carlton Winemakers Studio has an inviting tasting room.
Photograph by Andréa Johnson

Middle: The studio is defined by its collaborative winemaking talent.
Photograph by Clay McLachlan

Bottom: The rolling hills of the Yamhill-Carlton AVA provide a picturesque setting.
Photograph by Clay McLachlan

Facing Page: Guests are welcomed to the tasting room to enjoy wine and learn about the studio's eco-consciousness.
Photograph by Clay McLachlan

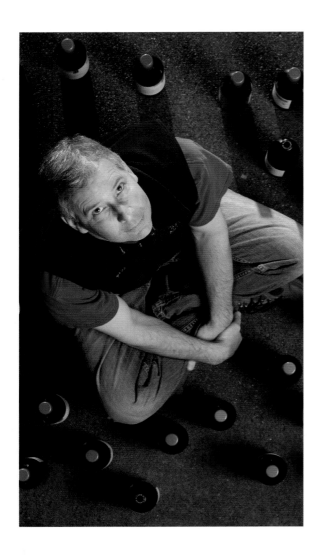

Andrew Rich Vintner

Carlton

One of the original vintners to join The Carlton Winemakers Studio when it opened in 2002, Andrew Rich is now a veteran of the collaborative winery incubator—he jokes that apparently he has yet to hatch. His love of wine was nurtured not in the fertile soils of the Willamette Valley, but in the urban sprawl of New York City, where he once edited the wine column for a national magazine. When the pull of wine became stronger than that of publishing, he headed to Burgundy to study winemaking and viticulture, a move that led to employment at the small but influential Bonny Doon Vineyard in California for nearly six years.

His skills honed, Andrew moved to Oregon in 1994 with the quixotic vision of making Rhône-style wines in the Willamette Valley from Columbia Valley grapes. Turns out he was a little ahead of the curve, and it wasn't until 2000, when grenache, mourvèdre, roussanne, and syrah grapes became available to him, that he was finally able to realize his vision.

Meanwhile, his love of pinot noir blossomed, and the fickle grape has since become his primary passion. There are three pinot blends, with fruit sourced from nearly a dozen northern Willamette Valley vineyards: the soft and approachable Prelude; the classic Verbatim, a "grape for grape translation of vintage and place"; and the structured and age-worthy Knife Edge.

While the range at Andrew Rich Wines may be broad—in addition to the pinots and Rhône-style wines, the winery is known for sauvignon blanc, gewürztraminer dessert wine, and several others—total production is a mere 6,000 cases.

Top: A rare moment of rest amid the hustle of harvest.

Bottom: Blending plays a crucial role, whether of different varietals—as in the Rhône-style wines—or of several vineyards, as in the pinots.
Photographs by Clay McLachlan

Asilda Wine

Carlton

Earl Lumpkins Sr. has always been a "lab guy." But when he applied his biology and chemistry background to inform the art of winemaking, he discovered a truly delicious specimen—and a veritable second career, although he prefers to call it a fun hobby.

It all started in 1994 with experiments at home, where he produced small batches of wine. His trial-and-error approach served him well. He now has a more fitting home to produce his Asilda Wine at The Carlton Winemakers Studio, which is partially owned by his cousin, Ned Lumpkin. Annually, he produces several hundred cases of pinot noir, sourced from his 11.5-acre Timbale & Thyme vineyard about three miles east of Carlton, Oregon, in the northern Willamette Valley.

Earl is not interested in quantity, only in quality. His relentless pursuit of extracting the most robust flavor from the blending of different clones is nearly palpable. It's certainly palate-pleasing, as his large, bold pinot noir wines are well-balanced with significant fruity notes, variously described as cherry and blackberry, along with espresso and dark chocolate.

As for the moniker of his wine, Earl originally picked Alchemy, which ultimately proved unavailable. Searching for another meaningful tie, he opted for Asilda, the name of his French-Canadian wife's great-aunt.

Top: Earl and Peggy Lumpkins.
Photograph by Andréa Johnson

Bottom: Picnic in the vineyard.
Photograph by Peggy Lumpkins

Bachelder

Carlton

"I want to make a Ferrari, not a Cadillac," exclaims winemaker Thomas Bachelder of his world-class, terroir-based wines from the cool-climate regions of Burgundy, France, as well as Niagara and Oregon—three places he has lived and loved. Together with his wife, Mary, he has been producing wine since the '90s. In 2009, he launched his namesake label, specializing in chardonnay and pinot noir.

Early on, Thomas discovered Burgundy, which prompted him to pursue winemaking at home, setting up cement vats and oak barrels in his Montreal basement. Later his passion led him to become a wine journalist and author.

However, it was his vigneron studies in Burgundy that really transformed his philosophy. Influenced by a Burgundian palate, he uniquely utilizes terroir winemaking to reveal the signature flavors of the Burgundy, Niagara, and Oregon grapes.

He takes particular pride in his chardonnay, where subtle use of the right barrels and long-oak aging yields a sinewy, broad, elegant—and ironically less oaky—wine. As for the pinot noir, his is defined by an explosive bouquet and rich mouthfeel. It has the "quirky ability to dance between black-flavored fruits and red-flavored berries in the same swallow," he says.

Encouraged by longtime friends and The Carlton Winemakers Studio co-owners, Luisa Ponzi and Eric Hamacher, Thomas joined the facility in 2011.

Top: Thomas Bachelder has always been at home in the cellar.
Photograph by Andréa Johnson

Middle: The Bachelder Willamette Valley Pinot Noir—Burgundian flair, Oregon flavors.
Photograph by Andréa Johnson

Bottom: Thomas helped rip the field and plant the Johnson Vineyard back in 2001, and is proud to be working with this great organic Lemelson fruit once again.
Photograph by Thomas Bachelder

Dukes Family Vineyards

Amity

For Jackie and Pat Dukes, the sharing of food and wine with friends has always been one of life's most rewarding joys. When they first came to Oregon from Phoenix, Arizona, visions of owning a restaurant were dancing in their heads, with Pat eager to put his Le Cordon Bleu culinary training to good use. But these would-be restaurateurs eventually steered their epicurean passion in another direction: winemaking.

It took the Dukes four years to find the right location for their vineyards. In 2005, their search ended with a beautiful, 58-acre property in the Eola-Amity Hills AVA of North Willamette Valley, where they also now live in a reconstructed barn that dates back to the 1870s.

The Dukes also have some history with The Carlton Winemakers Studio, as these enophiles first visited more than five years before planting their first grape, merely attracted to the sheer quantity of stylistic wine offerings in one place. Together with winemaking consultant Kelly Kidneigh, they crafted their 2010 vintage at Carlton and continue to utilize the facility, where they take a hands-on approach to produce boutique batches of high-quality pinot noir, as well as syrah and chardonnay.

Believing that great wine begins in the vineyard, Jackie and Pat are committed to low-impact, ecologically-sound farming methodology and the continual improvement of their vineyard environment. Not bad for a city couple, each on their second careers, who joke that they worked through their "midlife crises" together—with the help of wine, of course.

Top: It's just another day at the barn for Pat and Jackie Dukes, proprietors of Dukes Family Vineyards.
Photograph by Clay McLachlan

Middle: The historic 1870s barn is located in the Eola-Amity Hills AVA and overlooks the pond and vineyards.
Photograph by Jackie Dukes

Bottom: The reward at the end of the journey: Dukes Family Vineyards Alyssa Pinot Noir.
Photograph courtesy of Dukes Family Vineyards

Retour Winery

Carlton

Sixth-generation Oregonian Lindsay Woodard has been on a trailblazing path as a wine entrepreneur from an early age. Known for her steadfast ambition, she was one of the youngest individuals to start a winery in the Willamette Valley.

While attending Linfield College, she created the International Pinot Noir Celebration internship program. Upon earning her degree, she held an important position at Ponzi Vineyards and later ventured to Napa Valley. In 2004, she established Lindsay Woodard Communications, a branding and design firm, and continues to work with wineries, restaurants, and organizations around the world.

In 2005, with no fear of taking a risk, Lindsay founded Retour. "Retour is the French term for homecoming or returning home. I returned to my Oregon roots and set out to craft an exceptional old-vine pinot noir from highly acclaimed vineyards," she says. In collaboration with consulting winemaker Eric Hamacher, she crafts a complex wine that has earned copious accolades and has created a strong following among sommeliers and collectors.

Four years later, she established her second label, Manifest Destiny, as a tribute to her family who crossed The Oregon Trail in 1847. Their solid determination played a significant role in developing the western frontier and establishing Oregon as a state. "Manifest Destiny is about taking a risk and achieving one's full potential. It is a true reflection of the ideal American values, a celebration of independence, innovation, and exploration," Lindsay explains.

Relentless when it comes to perfection, she is known for her hands-on tending of the vines—even going so far as to pluck unwanted berries from clusters with tweezers. Her meticulous efforts create wines that matter, revealing the history, purity, and soul of the Willamette Valley.

Top: Lindsay Woodard is a sixth-generation Oregonian and the proprietor of Retour Winery.
Photograph by Carolyn Wells-Kramer

Bottom: Retour specializes in very limited production. The iconic metal label captures the distinct personality, purity, and eloquent structure of the wine.
Photograph by DL Images

Wahle Vineyards & Cellars

Portland

Much like the multiple branches of the grapevine, Mark Wahle's history of winemaking has been rich and varied, with a few twists and turns. His first brush with the vineyards actually began in high school when an educational project had him tending to his parents' property, Wahle Vineyards. Forerunners in their own right, they had planted the first commercial vineyard in the Yamhill-Carlton region of Oregon in 1974. After high school graduation, Mark continued his education at UC Davis, where he studied viticulture and enology.

Although he returned to his family's Oregon vines after school, he was soon also cultivating another career, attending medical school at UC Davis and later completing his residency at Charity Hospital in New Orleans, Louisiana. He currently splits his time between his emergency medicine practice in Portland and his grape-growing and winemaking passion.

Upon his return to Oregon, Mark broke ground for his second vineyard in 1999, a 310-acre site in the Eola Hills, which he calls Holmes Hill in honor of the property's homesteader. Embracing the different viticulture areas of these two estate vineyards, he is able to capitalize on unique wine expressions. The Yamhill-Carlton pinot noir is grown on sedimentary Willakenzie soil and often features mixed cherry, mushroom, and floral notes, while the Holmes Hill site and its volcanic Nekia soil yields notes of blackberry and pomegranate.

Something akin to destiny drove Mark to The Carlton Winemakers Studio in 2006. He and studio co-founder Eric Hamacher were once classmates at UC Davis nearly 20 years earlier, but hadn't connected since, so they barely recognized each other at a school parent-teacher conference. Good thing Eric was wearing his harvest boots.

Top: Mark Wahle during harvest at The Carlton Winemakers Studio.

Middle: The Wahle family at their Holmes Hill vineyard site.

Bottom: Wahle wine releases.
Photographs by Clay McLachlan

Chehalem

Newberg

Chehalem is a Native American word from the local Calapooia tribe best translated as "gentle land" or "valley of flowers," phrases that capture a long-standing, almost religious reverence for the land. The winery team understands this reverence, for they consider Chehalem to be a vineyard winery, dedicated to reflecting as purely as possible what the vineyard has produced, with minimal processing and without compromising great fruit. Plus, with estate vineyards located in three different AVAs, the diverse terroirs imbue Chehalem wines with a spectrum of unique flavors and aromas that proudly speak to special places. Chehalem traces its history back to vineyard operations started by Harry Peterson-Nedry in 1980 at Ridgecrest Vineyards, the pioneering wine operation on Ribbon Ridge, northwest of Newberg, Oregon. Bill and Cathy Stoller joined Harry in the winery in 1993 and subsequently began Stoller Vineyards—a densely planted 125 acres on Stoller family farmlands at the southern tip of the Dundee Hills. Corral Creek Vineyards, adjacent to the winery facility and in the Chehalem Mountains, is Chehalem's third estate vineyard. The winery's first release was the 1990 Ridgecrest Pinot Noir.

Crafting fine wine is a family affair at Chehalem. Second-generation winemaker Wynne Peterson-Nedry graduated with her master's in viticulture and enology from UC Davis, and in 2009, became Chehalem's assistant winemaker before being promoted to head winemaker in 2012. Wynne grew up around the grapevines and often spent summers in the vineyard at her father's side. Today she works alongside Harry to craft a broad array of precisely honed wines. With the help of assistant winemaker Katie Santora, a longtime friend of Wynne's, and the broadly talented and educated vineyard manager, Chad Douglas, the winemaking team collaborates on everything from vineyard practices for the current vintage to six-week snapshot technical tastings of the past cuvées in barrel and tank for tweaks and final blending.

Top: Harry Peterson-Nedry and Wynne Peterson-Nedry are the founding winemaker and current winemaker, respectively.

Bottom: The prime winemaker's motivation at harvest is driving the forklift.

Facing Page: Looking up the spine of Ribbon Ridge, the Wind Ridge Vineyards are below and Ridgecrest Vineyards above. Begun in 1980, these vineyards were Chehalem's first plantings and the first planted on what would become Ribbon Ridge AVA.
Photographs by Andrea Johnson

As co-owners, Harry and Bill appreciate the principle that great wines are grown, not made. With certifications from LIVE, Salmon-Safe, and the Oregon Certified Sustainable Wine program, Chehalem wines are crafted in an eco-friendly manner. The winery is committed to sustainability every step of the way, from planting to production. In the years since the first planting of Chehalem's Ridgecrest Vineyards in 1982, the winery has embraced sustainable farming techniques, worked to eliminate the use of petrochemical sprays and fertilizers, and made strides toward carbon neutrality through reduced bottle weights, on-demand water heating, insulation, and solar panel installations.

Chehalem's philosophy and style do not always follow the industry norms or market trends. That the team looks for deftness and elegance in pinot noirs at a time when black, opaque, extracted, and heavily wooded wines are the norm, speaks to this sense. That the winery crop-thins pinot gris as aggressively as pinot noir and looks for optimal ripeness, such that it is harvested after pinot noir, indicates an almost obsessive attention to detail. At a time when riesling is being pulled out, Chehalem counterintuitively plants prime acres to this variety, convinced it as sensitively reflects site and climate for white wine as pinot noir does for red. Small plantings of grüner veltliner and gamay noir also illustrate this stubborn, contrarian streak.

Above: Stoller Vineyards, the Dundee Hills AVA vineyard, serves as a Chehalem estate vineyard and the home of Stoller Family Estate, Chehalem's sister winery.

Left: With its contour plantings and solar panel arrays, Chehalem is nestled in the forest between Corral Creek Vineyards and Highway 99W.
Photographs by Andréa Johnson

Equally well-known for red and white-wine quality, Chehalem carries a passion and focus for cool climate varieties that reflect both site and climate in complex, structured, and intensely fruited wines. The winemaking team thinks their objective is not to follow today's trends, but to lead the way to a novel future that is stimulating, exciting, and beautiful—such as it must have been generations ago for the Calapooia, overlooking the "valley of flowers." Chehalem offers visitors a wide range of tasting and tour options, from library tastings by appointment at the winery to more casual walk-in tastings at the downtown Newberg tasting room, where guests are encouraged to explore the diverse portfolio of wines offered by Chehalem.

Above: The heart of Chehalem: the winery staff—dormant vines, passionately active personnel.

Left: Cellar barrel tasting and selection to craft single vineyard and reserve blends.

Facing Page: A family selection from the 18 wines Chehalem produces from pinot noir, riesling, chardonnay, pinot gris, grüner veltliner, pinot blanc, and gamay noir grape varieties.
Photographs by Andréa Johnson

Reserve Pinot Noir
Diverse pairings include game bird, salmon, lamb, and pork for this wine that demonstrates the wisdom of restraint.

Ian's Reserve Chardonnay
Exquisite with quiche, corn chowder, white meats, mushrooms, cream dishes, and more.

Corral Creek Riesling
An ideally balanced counterpoint for spicier fare like Thai curry, Szechuan, Tex-Mex, or Cajun.

Gamay Noir
Perfect for barbecue, wood-fired pizza, and charcuterie.

Tastings
Open to the public

CHEHALEM

Cherry Hill Winery

Rickreall

Full of wanderlust, it's no surprise that avid travelers Mike and Jan Sweeney began their life in the wine industry while on a trip to Burgundy. While biking through the beautiful French countryside, they met a couple from Portland, Oregon, who were intimately familiar with the wine industry in the Pacific Northwest. Once back in the US, Mike and Jan traveled from their home in Indiana to the slopes of the Willamette Valley to experience Oregon's wine at the source. While on a hike, they came across a beautiful plot of land at the top of a hill marked with a "for sale" sign. The sign derailed their wine tasting agenda, and Mike immediately made an offer on the land. Their future seemed to be held in the promise of that small sign and in the high-elevation vineyard. Fortunately, they were outbid and lost the property. It had been part of a champagne vineyard and wouldn't have produced their beloved pinot grapes.

The property sparked a search for other vineyards, though, this time with a little more research. Shortly thereafter, Mike, a farmer at heart, came across a gorgeous Royal Ann cherry orchard that was on the market. The Sweeneys won the bid and named the spot Cherry Hill Winery in honor of its prior orchards.

Today Cherry Hill, located in the Eola-Amity Hills AVA, is all about pinot noir, grown and produced under the careful eye of winemaker Ken Cook. Light red in color, the Cherry Hill Estate Pinot Noir is a supple, silky wine with a candied red cherry aroma and light tannins. The 2009 bottling of the flagship wine received 91 points from *Wine Spectator*, where it was described as fragrant, light, and a beautiful combination of ripe blueberry and plum flavors. Every bottle of Cherry Hill pinot puts the wine lover directly in touch with the lives of Mike and Jan. The Vanda Pinot Noir Dry Rosé, for instance, is decorated with a label featuring one of Jan's favorite orchids.

Top: Cherry Hill's pinot noir is a definite claim to fame.

Bottom: Proprietors Mike and Jan Sweeney are actively engaged in the winery's operations.

Facing Page: Belying the property's previous life as an orchard, the vineyards look as if they have always graced the landscape.
Photographs by Andréa Johnson

Perhaps the most delightful story can be found in the Dijon Cuvée Estate Pinot Noir. The wine is the particular favorite of Jan's Papillion, Daisy. She can be found anytime Ken and others check on the wine, which is made from a combination of three Dijon clones. The petite pooch—who was born with a white wine-glass-shaped spot on her forehead—anxiously waits for any leftover drops from the wine thief, the tube through which winemakers taste wine still in the barrel. Daisy apparently has discerning tastes, turning her nose up at barrels that she finds unacceptable. As a result, only the barrels that she selects go into the bottle. The extremely food-friendly wine features fresh berry flavors, with hints of spice and caramel, and a mellow finish.

In honor of the winery's heritage and Oregon's cherry farming history, Cherry Hill also private-labels luxurious dark chocolate-covered cherries. Made from Royal Ann cherries, the candies are produced just a few miles away from the winery. The cherries are a favorite of Jan's when it comes to food pairings for Cherry Hill pinot noir; her passion lies in cooking and entertaining. She is continually coming up with new recipes to feature at winemaker's dinners.

Left: From vineyards to cellar to terrace, Cherry Hill offers visitors a wonderful variety of scenery and experiences.
Photographs by Andréa Johnson

Visitors are invited to sample and purchase the Sweeney Reserve Pinot Noir, a wine that is selected by Mike from his favorite barrels of estate fruit and is available at the winery only. The 100-percent Pommard clone-based wine is the holy grail of the vineyard—the absolute best of the best that Cherry Hill has to offer. Small group barrel tastings and winemaker's dinners are available by appointment. Friends of the winery are invited to stay at one of the quaint cabins overlooking the grapevines, each built from native Oregon wood. A stroll in the vineyard, with its sweeping views of the surrounding Eola Hills, and a chat with the winemaker is a great way to end the tour.

Above, Left & Facing Page: The Sweeneys love nothing more than sharing their passion with visitors. Throughout the estate, there are many backdrops for formal wine education, casual conversations, multisensory tastings, and lively dinner parties.
Photographs by Andréa Johnson

Cherry Hill Estate Pinot Noir
Pair with grilled salmon, braised beef, lamb, or chocolate.

Dijon Cuvée Estate Pinot Noir
Elegant alongside hearty pasta dishes.

Cherry Hill Blanc de Noir
Serve with lightly sauced pasta or fresh, light seafood.

Vanda Pinot Noir Dry Rosé
Pairs beautifully with spicy Asian dishes and light seafood dishes.

Tastings
Open to the public, seasonally

Cherry Hill Winery

Estate Pinot Noir

Willamette Valley
Eola - Amity Hills

Christopher Bridge Cellars

Oregon City

Twenty-five miles south of Portland, you'll find 80 pristine acres with beautiful views of the Williamette Valley. This piece of land cast its magical spell on Ragnhild and Wolfgang Carlberg in 1952, when the first-generation American couple bought the homestead and began farming it. Their five-year-old son, Chris, took a liking to it immediately, spending time playing and exploring in the fields and forest that quilt the hillside. Even then he understood that a heartfelt connection with the land and its wild inhabitants was a source of physical and emotional nourishment.

After 30 years of teaching in Oregon and Germany, Chris returned to the family farm with his wife, Susanne. With encouragement from his sister and brother-in-law, the couple planted 3,600 vinifera vines and established Satori Springs Vineyard in 1998. The first wines of the Christopher Bridge label were produced in 2001 at his brother-in-law's Vashon Winery. By 2007, Chris and Susanne had expanded the vineyard to 15 acres and established a winery on the estate next to their home. Chris became a full-time grower and winemaker.

A self-admitted contemplative person, Chris explains that the word "bridge" in the winery's name expresses both a poignant journey into a new endeavor as well as meaningful relationships. He carefully tends the farm, planting trees, raising cattle, and providing for wildlife, while slowly expanding his vineyard and a following for his wines. He believes that to craft a rewarding wine includes a good land ethic, one that speaks of sustainability, harmony, beauty, and hospitality. "Wine is an experience with all its mysteries and the memories it can create. It is music in the mouth," he says. The Carlbergs don't just live on the land, they live with it. This dedication can be tasted in every glass of wine they pour.

Top: Chris and Susanne Carlberg enjoy sharing the farm with their companion, Dexter.
Photograph by Andréa Johnson

Middle: Beautiful Willamette Valley views to the south, west, and north beckon from the tasting room and deck.
Photograph by Susanne Carlberg

Bottom: A time capsule of Satori Springs Vineyard and the enduring experiences of its stewards.
Photograph by Andréa Johnson

Facing Page: Good taste and hospitality go hand in hand in the tasting room.
Photograph by Andréa Johnson

Coelho Winery

Amity

The story of Coelho Winery begins in California's beautiful San Joaquin Valley, where Dave and Deolinda Coelho farmed 800 acres of alfalfa, tomatoes, sugar beets, and corn, but they looked to relocate and begin a new venture. In 1990, a family camping trip north to Oregon, Washington, and Idaho yielded a new love for the Willamette Valley and particularly for the little town of Amity, Oregon. It made sense then for Dave and Deolinda to seek out land to cultivate their dream of a specialized crop, most notably premium grapes. The estate property, purchased in 1991, is now the vineyard that sprawls across 40 rolling acres of former wheat fields.

The family's love of winemaking began generations before the first vintage bottling of Paciência in 2004: Both Dave and Deolinda's grandfathers made wine either experimentally or as a hobby. This love continues with today's generation, making the business truly a family affair. Dave and Deolinda's sons, David and Samuel, take an active role in the winery's daily operations. Since 2002, David and Samuel have enthusiastically gotten down in the Willamette Valley dirt, cultivating the soil with the utmost respect for its natural state. After years in the vineyards and their respective college experiences, David became the head winemaker at Coelho Winery in 2010, and Samuel returned to lead the marketing and branding department. Together with their sisters, Stephanie and Jeanne, who offer their creativity in marketing and label design decisions, David and Samuel are continuing their family's tradition of winemaking.

Top: Coelho Winery's five-year barrel-aged port-style wine.

Bottom: Paciência Reserva Pinot Noir is a family favorite.

Facing Page: Coelho Estate Vineyard is breathtaking in midsummer.
Photographs by Andréa Johnson

Hand-picked and hand-sorted, the grapes at Coelho Winery are grown under the attentive eye of the entire team. Kestrel boxes strategically placed throughout the vineyard encourage birds of prey to settle on the vineyard's slopes, providing natural rodent control. Roses planted at the end of the rows help Dave and the rest of the growers ascertain the state of the vineyard, detecting potential insect infestations at the earliest possible time. Grass is planted between the rows to increase the stress on the vines, thereby producing berries of smaller size but larger flavor.

The winery produces a variety of wines that pay homage to the family's Portuguese heritage. The Tradição Portuguese Red Wine, named for the Portuguese word for tradition, embodies the rich, full-bodied qualities of Old World wines. Aromas of wild berries, spring flowers, and tropical fruits join an earthiness that reflects the terroir of the vineyard site. Likewise, the Aventura Port is crafted in what David calls the vintage port style. A combination of sweet fruit aromas and floral notes come together before a delicious wood spice finish. In true European style, Aventura Port is beautiful alongside gourmet food selections or when enjoyed alone.

The Coelho family's love of the region extends beyond these green rows of beautiful pinot noir, pinot gris, and chardonnay grapes and the wines they make. In 2003, the family purchased a circa-1930 hardware store that had sat abandoned in Amity to serve as the winery's production facility and welcome center. The building suffered from a fire in the 1970s, but when the Coelhos renovated it, they left the beams—which were charred but structurally sound—as they found them, adding a rustic, thoroughly Oregonian feel to the space. Old floorboards from a 1920s-era grainery, and furniture created by local artisans, welcome visitors on a daily basis to sample the winery's sustainably produced wine.

Left: Samuel, Dave, David, and Deolinda Coelho showcase one aspect of their family winery.
Photograph by Andréa Johnson

Hand in hand with promoting the winery is the promotion of the town of Amity itself. As one of the founders of the Amity Downtown Improvement Group, otherwise known as Amity DIG, Deolinda works to create a unified and defined downtown space within the community. Through leadership programs to promote a vital rural community, Deolinda and the rest of the Amity DIG team host fundraising events, a holiday tree lighting, movies in the park, and even a circus held at Amity City Park. Fueled by tradition and passionate about wine, the Coelho family continues to be forward-thinking both in the industry and the community that embraces it.

Above: David, Samuel, Deolinda, and Dave converted a historical hardware store in downtown Amity into their family's tasting room.

Left: Customers enjoy visiting with Coelho's educated staff.

Facing Page: David and Samuel thieve a barrel sample of the Coelho Estate Vineyard Pinot Noir in their cellar.
Photographs by Andréa Johnson

WINE & FARE

Paciência Reserva Estate Pinot Noir
Pairs beautifully with bone-in filet mignon, balsamic roasted vegetables, and dark chocolate.

Renovação Estate Pinot Gris
Serve alongside ginger grilled shrimp or light pasta dishes.

Apreciação Estate Chardonnay
Elegantly pairs with lobster and drawn butter, served alongside spring salads.

Aventura Portuguese Varietal 5 Year Port
Enjoy with chocolate fudge or Stilton cheese.

Tastings
Open to the public daily

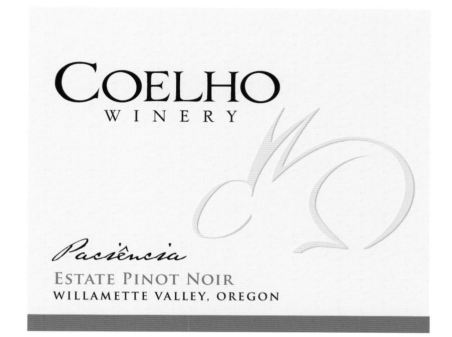

COELHO
W I N E R Y

Paciência
ESTATE PINOT NOIR
WILLAMETTE VALLEY, OREGON

Cubanisimo Vineyards

Willamette Valley

A native of Havana, Cuba, Mauricio Collada Jr. came to the United States in 1962. Later he became fascinated with wine while he was a student in the pre-med program at the University of Miami in Florida, where he made wine from mangoes and bananas. His interest in winemaking continued throughout medical school.

When Mauricio arrived in Oregon in 1983 to start his medical practice and establish his family, he was pleasantly surprised to discover that his favorite wine grape, pinot noir, had the perfect climatic conditions for its development in the Willamette Valley. Three years later, he purchased a 21-acre parcel in the Eola-Amity Hills, and Cubanisimo Vineyards was born.

The name Cubanisimo pays homage to Mauricio's native country, as it translates to "very Cuban." From the beginning of the winery, Mauricio and his staff have been committed to creating a top quality product meriting the name. Initially he focused on refining the vineyard's management, as he sold grapes to larger Oregon wineries such as King Estate and Erath. Through Cubanisimo's relationship with Erath, Mauricio met Rob Stuart—a serendipitous occasion, as Rob became the vineyard's winemaker.

By 2003, Cubanisimo began keeping half of its grape production to produce its own wines, which resulted in 540 cases. Two years later when its vineyard and winery contracts expired, Cubanisimo kept all of its grapes, and the construction of wine tasting facilities began. At the same time, Mauricio slowly began adding to the vineyard's plantings.

Top: Cubanisimo wines are meant to be enjoyed at any occasion.
Photograph by Andréa Johnson

Bottom: Owners Debra and Mauricio Collada celebrate at home.
Photograph by Andréa Johnson

Facing Page: The estate is majestically situated on the Cubanisimo property.
Photograph: courtesy of Cubanisimo Vineyards

In 2004 when Debra, a nurse, met Mauricio, she also discovered her fascination for wine. She now splits her time between her nursing career and Cubanisimo, where she walks the vineyards with Mauricio, participates with the harvest and bottling of the wines, and dedicates herself to all other aspects of the vineyard as its event coordinator. Together they continue to grow the winery and maintain the high quality of its wines.

Cubanisimo's vineyards face southeast from a 650-foot elevation that offers breathtaking views of Willamette Valley. The vineyard currently produces 800 cases of Estate Pinot Noir yearly and another 1,000 cases that blend its estate grapes with other pinot noir grapes sourced from other vineyards in the valley.

Extracting the finest elements nature will yield from the grapes and the terroir are at the heart of Cubanisimo's winemaking philosophy. The fine balance of stress and nurture achieved by the five-by-seven-foot spacing of its plantings, and the absence of irrigation adds a complexity and depth of flavor to its pinots that guests enjoy visit after visit.

Top: A Cuban sandwich, croquettes, black beans, rice, and Cubanisimo wines are a simple delight.
Photograph by Andrèa Johnson

Bottom: Cubanisimo Vineyards shows commitment to excellence in every bottle.
Photograph by Andrèa Johnson

Facing Page: The gardens outside the tasting room are beautiful.
Photograph courtesy of Cubanisimo Vineyards

Estate Pinot Noir
An elegant pinot noir to enjoy with salmon or Mediterranean cuisine.

Rumba Pinot Noir
The best partner for an evening of salsa dancing or an afternoon family barbecue.

Pinot Gris
Magnificent with seafood, Asian food, and salads of all sorts.

Rosado de Pinot Noir
The perfect summertime wine that pairs easily with seafood, chicken, or pork.

Tastings
Open to the public, seasonally

Domaine Drouhin Oregon
Dayton

In 1987, Robert Drouhin of Burgundy's Maison Joseph Drouhin purchased land in the Dundee Hills of Oregon. It was a watershed moment for the young Oregon wine industry and its visionary pioneers. Robert's own foresight helped confirm the region's potential for growing exceptional pinot noir and built a permanent bridge between Burgundy and the Willamette Valley.

After establishing Domaine Drouhin Oregon, Robert's first order of business was to task his daughter, Véronique, with the winemaking at their new Oregon venture. Véronique had earned a master's degree in enology from the Université de Bourgogne in Dijon in France, and spent the 1986 harvest in the Willamette Valley, working with three of the pioneering families of Oregon wine. As a Drouhin, Véronique grew up with wine and learned to taste seriously from a young age. She has, quite literally, a lifetime of experience.

Philippe Drouhin, Véronique's older brother, was given responsibility for viticulture starting in 1988 and is in charge of the family's estates in Burgundy and Oregon. His focus on finding natural answers for natural problems is why all of their estate holdings in Burgundy are certified organic, and why the Oregon vineyards are LIVE certified sustainable. He holds degrees from the École Supérieure du Commerce Extérieur, an international business school in France, and the Lycée Viticole de Beaune, a school of viticulture, and like Véronique, studied enology at the Université de Bourgogne.

Top: Véronique Drouhin-Boss is the winemaker.
Photograph by Andréa Johnson

Bottom & Facing Page: The winery is a four-level, gravity-flow landmark tucked into the hillside.
Photographs by Serge Chapuis

Domaine Drouhin Oregon's first vintage was 1988, which happened to be an excellent year. This helped convince the Drouhins to accelerate their commitment in Oregon, and in February of 1989 they broke ground on what is now considered an Oregon landmark— an elegant, four-level, gravity-flow winery set into the Dundee Hills. At the same time, they planted high-density vineyards, which were three to four times denser than what was then standard in Oregon. And, critically, Domaine Drouhin Oregon was the first winery in the state to plant using phylloxera-resistant rootstock, a measure that ensures the vines will reach old age.

In 1992, Domaine Drouhin Oregon released its first special pinot noir barrel selection, which was named for Véronique's firstborn daughter, Laurène. The wine is made each year from the top barrels in the cellar and has become iconic in Oregon and beyond. In 1999, Véronique created Louise, an even more limited and collectable barrel selection named for her younger daughter. Domaine Drouhin Oregon's estate chardonnay was renamed Arthur in 2002, for Véronique's son. The chardonnay vines were planted in 1992, just after Domaine Drouhin Oregon received some of the first Dijon clones in the state. In recent years, Véronique has developed an Edition Limitée series for small lot selections, and each summer visitors to the winery look forward to Edition Rosé, made entirely from pinot noir.

Left: A sunrise view of the Drouhin estate, overlooking the Willamette Valley
Photograph by Andréa Johnson

Today Domaine Drouhin Oregon sits on a 225-acre estate, with 124 acres under vine in the Dundee Hills. The Drouhin family also recently purchased Roserock, a beautiful vineyard in the Eola-Amity Hills AVA. Véronique has become internationally recognized for her winemaking, while her brother Philippe is equally well-regarded for his viticulture skills. Domaine Drouhin Oregon's vineyards and winery are both LIVE certified sustainable, and the property maintains one of the largest solar panel arrays of any Oregon winery. Most importanty, the wines have earned their reputation for excellence and age-worthiness.

Domaine Drouhin Oregon is open year-round, with private tours and tastings by appointment.

Above: Philippe Drouhin and vineyard manager Tim Scott discuss the coming harvest.
Photograph by Andréa Johnson

Left: Tours of the winery conclude with a seated comparative tasting of Drouhin wines from Oregon and Burgundy.
Photograph by Serge Chapuis

Facing Page: The deck features extraordinary views of the estate's oldest blocks.
Photograph by Serge Chapuis

WINE & FARE

Arthur Chardonnay
Pair with Dungeness crab, corn beignets, sole almondine, and lobster bisque.

Dundee Hills Pinot Noir
Perfect alongside Gougère and French cheeses like Comté, Tomme de Savoie, and Saint Nectaire.

Lauréne Estate Pinot Noir
Savor with oeufs en meurette (eggs poached in red wine), wild mushroom risotto, or magrets de canard aux cerises (duck breast with cherries).

Louise Estate Pinot Noir
Delicious with roasted rack of lamb and savory boeuf bourguignon.

Tastings
Open to the public

Domaine Drouhin
OREGON

Domaine Margelle
Vineyards

Scotts Mills

Love at first sight… That's what happened to Marci and Steven Taylor when they first saw the property that would become Domaine Margelle Vineyards. Located in the Cascade foothills of the Willamette Valley, Domaine Margelle captured the essence of the Taylors' interests: an endless view reminiscent of the French countryside they had explored extensively, a microclimate similar to Burgundy to help create the style of wines the Taylors prefer, and proximity to the food and wine mecca of Portland.

The Willamette Valley is known for chardonnay, pinot gris, and pinot noir, and Domaine Margelle is no exception. Stonewall Estate, as the name translates, consists of 30 acres of vines planted in rocky Nekia soil that give the wines their bright, mineral flavors. Situated at an elevation between 800 and 900 feet, with a southwestern exposure and cool winds to allow the fruit maximum hang time, the vines create well-balanced flavors. Once harvested, the pinot gris is processed in stainless steel tanks and the pinot noir is aged in French oak barrels. In every bottle, you find a lovely nose and layered flavors; a reflection of the terroir unique to Domaine Margelle.

The real treat is the property itself; an example of Old World sentiment that speaks to the Taylor family's sensibility. To experience the royal treatment, join the exclusive wine club and be one of those lucky enough to discover the magic that is Domaine Margelle Vineyards.

Top: The property's pump house looks like a Provencial "petit mas" and makes a lovely spot to sit and enjoy a glass of Domaine Margelle wine.
Photograph by Val Lemings Photography

Middle: An iron trellis is the inspiration for Domaine Margelle's label and marks a footpath entrance through the stone wall and into the vineyard.
Photograph by Ray Nelson

Bottom: The Old World-style fountain welcomes guests to the property.
Photograph by Val Lemings Photography

Facing Page: Every room of the private estate looks out over the pond and has a commanding view of the vineyard, Willamette Valley, and the mountains beyond.
Photograph by Andréa Johnson

Domaine Serene

Dayton

Founded in 1989 by Ken and Grace Evenstad, Domaine Serene—named after their daughter—has quickly become one of Oregon's iconic producers of world-class pinot noir and chardonnay. The Evenstads' mission to produce consistently exquisite pinot noir has allowed Domaine Serene to become a recognized leader in the Oregon wine industry. Wine writers have called Domaine Serene the benchmark for domestic pinot noir and the Château Lafite Rothschild of Oregon. Domaine Serene holds the honor of having the highest rated pinot noir in Oregon, and in 2013, *Wine Spectator* ranked the Evenstad Reserve Pinot Noir number three in the world.

Domaine Serene's Winery Hill Estate, located in the heart of the prestigious Red Hills of Dundee in the northern Willamette Valley, houses one of the world's most advanced winemaking facilities; a five-level, state-of-the-art, gravity-flow winery. From the very beginning, Domaine Serene has focused on excellence. From hand-sorting all incoming grapes to over-vintaging the wines in barrel, the Evenstad's passion for quality in the vineyards and in the bottle is unwavering. The vineyards of this site face east, south, and west, with glorious views of the Cascade Mountains, the Coast Range, and the Willamette Valley. Varying clones, rootstocks, microclimates, slope, and elevation allow for the creation of distinct and complex wines with every vintage.

Top: Grace and Ken Evenstad are living the American dream as proprietors of Domaine Serene.
Photograph by Carolyn Kramer Wells

Middle: The modern gravity-flow winery was completed in 2001, just in time for harvest.
Photograph courtesy of Domaine Serene

Bottom & Facing Page: Domaine Serene utilizes sustainable farming practices and insists on low yields to ensure maximum expression of the terroir.
Photograph by Carolyn Kramer Wells

Elizabeth Chambers Cellar

McMinnville

"It may be because I am a woman, but I am not interested in seeing who can make the wine with the biggest muscles," says owner Elizabeth Chambers. "I want to drink wines that have table manners, wines that can dance. I want elegance and style in my wines." It is this philosophy that has ultimately emerged from Liz's winemaking journey that began when her mother, Carolyn Chambers, acquired Hinman Vineyards in 1993, which became the Silvan Ridge Winery. Just two short years later, Liz, a finance professional and third generation Oregonian who previously managed risks and benefits for another family business, the Chambers Communications Corporation, was learning the ropes of an entirely new industry.

While she will be the first to admit that it was not always an easy road, her shrewd management of Silvan Ridge eventually evolved into a passion, prompting her to purchase another winery, Panther Creek, in 2005. It was a turning point for Liz, who discovered just how much she loved pinot noir in the process. This North Willamette Valley location evolved into her namesake winery, Elizabeth Chambers Cellar, which launched with its 2011 Pinot Noir. With the expertise of winemaker Michael Stevenson and associate winemaker JP Valot, the boutique cellar crafts a maximum of 3,000 cases, including single-vineyard designations that set the winery's top-quality pinot noirs apart.

As for the signature blue butterfly on each wine label, it represents Liz's mother, who collected the pretty winged creatures. After all, it was Carolyn's own passion for the vineyard that ultimately inspired her daughter. The tasting room is open daily from 12pm-5pm.

Top: Owner Elizabeth Chambers is passionate about wine.
Photograph by Andréa Johnson

Middle: Located close to Yamhill, Lazy River Vineyard lies on a bench of well-drained Jory soil—unusual outside of the Dundee Hills—resulting in complex, supple pinot noir.
Photograph by Andréa Johnson

Bottom: Winemaker Michael Stevenson enjoys his dogs, Bailey and Frankie.
Photograph courtesy of Elizabeth Chambers Cellar

Facing Page: Elizabeth Chambers Cellar is located in the heart of McMinnville Granary District in the historic power station building.
Photograph by Andréa Johnson

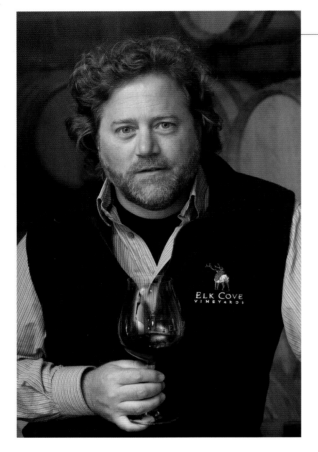

Elk Cove Vineyards

Gaston

In the misty morning that lingered over a protected cove in Gaston, Oregon, 50 migratory elk wandered onto the site of an abandoned homestead recently acquired by Pat and Joe Campbell. From their temporary trailer, the Campbell family watched the majestic creatures graze in the green grass. That day, the name of their future winery was realized: Elk Cove Vineyards.

Winemaking is a family affair at Elk Cove. From the start, Pat used the knowledge gleaned from growing up on a pear farm to oversee the vineyard management. Joe could be found among the freshly picked grapes and oak barrels, making wine. Today their son Adam Campbell—with the help of associate winemaker Heather Perkin—crafts a wide range of wines, including an elegant trinity of pinot varietals: pinot blanc, pinot gris, and pinot noir.

From the first vintage in 1977, the winery has produced single-vineyard pinot noirs in addition to other varietals. Adam and his team tailor vine yields using shoot thinning, severe pruning, and green harvesting techniques, which yield complex berries with dense juice that is then gently fermented at Elk Cove's gravity-flow winery. Elk Cove spans 250 scenic acres, and all five of the hillside vineyards are sustainably farmed with cover crops that amend the soil and prevent erosion.

Top: Adam Campbell is both owner and winemaker.
Photograph by Anna M. Campbell

Bottom: Elk Cove's Mount Richmond Vineyard is planted with a lush cover crop of red clover.
Photograph by Andréa Johnson

Facing Page: The estate and vineyards are beautifully nestled in the scenic countryside.
Photograph by Andréa Johnson

Hand-selected and blended from an exclusive number of vineyard blocks, the grapes that go into the Pinot Noir Reserve make the wine an elegant example of craftsmanship. Its perfumed aromatics, intense palate, and long, luxurious finish make it an indulgence. Robert Parker's *The Wine Advocate* described the oak-fermented, bright red 2008 bottling as "satin on the tongue."

The winery also produces cold-climate whites carefully fermented in small stainless steel tanks. Riesling crafted from the estate vineyard boasts a crisp acidity with aromas of lemongrass and kumquat. Balanced and delightfully dry, the riesling is a food-friendly wine that is equally as enjoyable alone.

Above: Two cherished hens accompany the Campbell family: Carrie, Pat, Adam, and Joe with children Georgia, Francis, and Silas.
Photograph by Andrea Johnson

Right: Ripe pinot noir grapes welcome the morning dew.
Photograph by Anna M. Campbell

Facing Page: The vineyards produce luscious fruits and full-bodied wines.
Photograph by Andrea Johnson

Elk Cove Vineyards is more than just a producer of distinctive wines; the Campbells support a number of nonprofit organizations. Elk Cove produces and bottles the annually selected wine for Condor Wines Northwest, a program that benefits hunger relief in the Cayma district of Arequipa, Peru. Other organizations include Salud!, an annual event geared toward providing health care services for seasonal vineyard workers; Friends of the Columbia Gorge; and the Oregon chapter of the Make-A-Wish Foundation.

Family, philanthropy, and fine wine are the standards of Elk Cove Vineyards, where an integration of nature and meticulous winemaking techniques creates wines reflective of the northern Willamette Valley. The diversity of wines that extends beyond the Oregon staple of pinot noir sets Elk Cove apart. Its pinot gris, pinot noir rosé, riesling, and sparkling wine illustrate the scope of the Campbells' winemaking artistry and their true passion for wine.

Visitors to Elk Cove Vineyards enjoy breathtaking views of the Pacific Coast Range mountains while sipping on ruby reds and crystal-clear whites in the naturally lit tasting room. Robert Parker Jr. noted its peerless beauty in *The Wine Advocate*: "Where tall windows and large outdoor decks present a serene landscape that evokes peaceful contemplation."

Top: Visitors enjoy the tasting room's memorable view.
Photograph by Anna M. Campbell

Middle: Joe and Pat planted their first grapevine in 1974.
Photograph courtesy of Elk Cove Vineyards

Bottom: Fred and Klas water young pinot noir vines using then-state-of-the-art machines and processes.
Photograph by Joe Campbell

Facing Page: Nothing is as picturesque as sunrise at Elk Cove's Five Mountain Vineyard during harvest.
Photograph by Anna M. Campbell

Pinot Noir Willamette Valley
Pairs beautifully with roasted duck or wild mushroom pastas.

Pinot Gris
Pairs elegantly with grilled trout and spring greens.

Estate Riesling
Perfect alongside pad Thai or spicy shrimp skewers.

Tastings
Open to the public daily

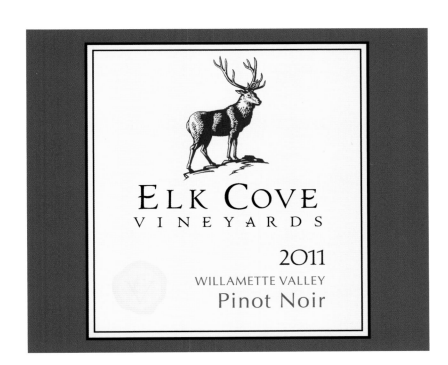

ELK COVE
VINEYARDS

2011

WILLAMETTE VALLEY
Pinot Noir

Erath Winery

Dundee

Like so many Oregon pinot pioneers, Dick Erath began making wine in his garage. The year was 1965, and the idea of making wine in the state was still an outlandish concept to many, yet Dick immediately saw the terroir's potential. Just three years later, he purchased his first vineyard site in the Chehalem Mountains and, in 1969, more than 20 wine varieties—including four acres of pinot noir—had been planted. Since that time, the stylistic statement of Erath Winery wines has been consistent: pinots that are silky, elegant, a little more European in style, and very fresh in fruit. The legacy of Erath Winery is not only the luxurious wines produced annually, but the integral role that Dick has played in the development of the Oregon wine industry.

Winemakers throughout the region cite Dick as one of the helping hands they received when starting their own wineries. Vineyards across the Willamette Valley are integrated with French clones introduced to the soil by his hand. In fact, Erath Winery, as the first winery in Dundee Hills, stands as a monument to the establishment of the Oregon wine industry. The innovative spirit that provided the impetus to found Erath Winery continues today.

Winemaker Gary Horner, who came on board in 2003, brings technology to tradition by applying Pneumatage to the craft of winemaking. Pneumatage is the injection of a large bubble of air into the bottom of the fermentor, gently mixing the fermenting grapes without crushing them. Pneumatage is just one step in Gary's overall very gentle processing approach with the goal of soft-extraction always in mind. Erath wines are all about the essence of the fruit, never about squeezing everything out of the berries. The result is consistent, luxurious, and affordable wine.

Top: Erath Winery's tasting room welcomes guests daily.

Bottom: Gary Horner has long served as winemaker.

Facing Page: Erath Winery's Knight's Gambit Vineyard.
Photographs by Andréa Johnson

KNIGHT'S GAMBIT
VINEYARD

AN ERATH VINEYARDS
GRAPE GROWER

Erath's Oregon tier wines are soft, fruit forward wines with no rough edges. The Oregon Pinot Noir boasts aromas of red plum, raspberry, spice, and soft sage, with juicy Bing cherry, cranberry cocktail, and a hint of vanilla spice delighting the palate. The sunny Oregon Pinot Blanc offers flavors of apple, melon, and lemon zest with a fresh finish. Fragrances of rose petals and honeydew characterize the Oregon Pinot Gris. Its flavors of lemon and green apple with a hint of banana make the wine absolutely mouthwatering. The Estate Selection Pinot Noir features the best of what the multiple estate vineyards have to offer. The bottling changes yearly, depending upon the climate conditions, but the taste is consistent and true to the Erath style: soft, luxurious cool-climate wines.

Above: Harvest at Erath's Prince Hill Vineyard.

Left: The view to the east from the Dundee Hills.

Facing Page: The view to the south from the Dundee Hills.
Photographs by Andréa Johnson

Oregon Pinot Noir
Pairs beautifully with grilled scallops in a Thai pepper sauce or zesty barbecue.

Oregon Pinot Blanc
Serve alongside grilled seafood, mild cheeses, and crudités.

Oregon Pinot Gris
Pairs well with Asian-spiced shellfish or spicy pork.

Erath Winery Estate Selection Pinot Noir
Elegant alongside roast duck with wild mushrooms and chocolate.

Tastings
Open to the public daily

J.K. Carriere

Newberg

Jim Prosser's four-year-old quips, "He doesn't make money, he makes wine." Not perfect, but the sentiment is close. Jim's actual mantra: "Make the wine first." Raised on skis in Bend, Oregon, and after stints in the corporate world and the Peace Corps, Jim sought to satisfy his intrigue of winemaking. Across four countries he found skilled craft, hard work, and low wages, two of which brought a smile every day. Nine wineries and nearly 20 years later, it still does.

Since bootstrapping J.K. Carriere in 1999, Jim has been recognized as producing some of the most acid-driven and age-able pinot noirs in the US. He's the one farming the hill organically, whose hands are winemaking—natural—and whose eyes ensure the care of great Oregon vineyard sources—Anderson Family, Gemini, JKC Estate, Shea, Temperance Hill. He tells stories via liquid in bottle. You gain access by visiting and pulling a cork.

In 2009, Jim built a new winery on Parrett Mountain, outside Newberg. There you'll find a barn of this century, with caves dug into the red cobble and a giant wasp appended to the exterior; the wasp is their logo and also a deadly allergy for Jim. The winery is flanked by vineyards, in turn surrounded by forest, with a view that looks towards the Cascade Range. You won't mistake it, or the winemaker, for anywhere else but Oregon. The tasting room is open Friday and Saturday, March through November, and by appointment.

Top: J.K. Carriere's modern barn and vineyards are nestled among the trees on beautiful Parrett Mountain, in the Chehalem Mountains AVA.
Photograph by Andréa Johnson

Bottom: Owner and winemaker Jim Prosser pays homage to the wasps that can kill him by placing them on both his winery and his wine labels.
Photograph by Andréa Johnson

Facing Page: J.K. Carriere's new smart and small winery represents Oregon, using simple and local materials in unique ways, including wine caves made of metal highway culverts.
Photograph by William E. Enos/Emerald Light

Kramer Vineyards

Gaston

In 1970, Trudy Kramer purchased a winemaking book and made her first gallon of wine. Thus began a major quest to discover the complexities of winemaking. In 1980, she took a wine appreciation class with Matt Kramer, an American wine critic of no relation. Trudy left the class with a better understanding of wine, as well as the goal of making a pinot noir as fine as the Burgundies she had tasted there. In 1984, she and her husband, Keith, bought some hillside property in Gaston, where they planted grapes and now farm more than 20 acres of vines.

Keith, a retired pharmacist and vice president of Kramer Vineyards, manages the site, assists in winemaking, and pitches in on busy weekends pouring wine. Trudy, president and CEO, has continued her involvement in winemaking, but spends much of her time focused on accounting and planning. Having grown up at the vineyard, Trudy and Keith's daughter, Kim, didn't tap into her winemaking aspirations until after college. She took a wine appreciation class at Chemeketa Community College and was hooked. Later, she took winemaking classes at the new Chemeketa Viticulture Center in Salem.

In 2006, Kim successfully made her first experimental batch of sparkling wine from an excess amount of chardonnay from St. Innocent. Three years later, she made her sparkling winemaking debut with Kramer Vineyards' 2009 vintage. Kim is now the resident winemaker at Kramer Vineyards. In 2010, Kim traveled to France to work harvest at Domaine AF Gros-Parent in Burgundy, a family with a winemaking history going back 13 generations. An amazing experience, she brought home techniques that were quickly implemented.

Top: Keith, Trudy, and Kim Kramer are passionate proprietors.

Bottom: Carmine is one of the rare varieties grown at Kramer Vineyards.

Facing Page: The 20-acre estate vineyard is located in the northern part of the Yamhill-Carlton AVA in the Willamette Valley.
Photographs by Andréa Johnson

Located in the northern part of the Yamhill-Carlton AVA in the Willamette Valley, the pristine environment of the vineyard allows the Kramer family to nurture their grapes to the fullest extent. The surrounding forest is filled with diverse populations of plants and animals. Each part of the land is put to its best use in order for the vineyard's ecosystem to thrive. The vineyard has been LIVE certified sustainable since 2005.

Kramer Vineyards' tasting room offers delightful wines of excellent quality, terrific value, and variety. The wines are served with a warm, inviting approach. Often guests can meet members of the family or their staff who have had direct involvement in producing the wine—eagerly sharing the story of the sparkling wine or the pinot noir, as they believe this knowledge only enhances the winery experience. Although the family has more than a 30-year relationship with the land, no vintage is ever the same. For the Kramers, winemaking is a process that should constantly evolve.

Above: Winemaker Kim Kramer assists with harvest.

Left: Sparkling wine is a specialty at Kramer Vineyards.

Facing Page: All of the grapes are meticulously harvested by hand.
Photographs by Andréa Johnson

Sparkling Wines
Pair with a wide range of fare, such as appetizers, quiche, salty foods, or sushi.

Pinot Noir Estate
Complements foods with earthy flavors, especially mushrooms or game. Enjoy with roasted duck, grilled salmon, rack of lamb, or tuna.

Chardonnay Estate
Serve with dishes that have butter, cream, or cheese, such as roasted salmon with a lemon sauce, coquilles St. Jacques, crab cakes, or linguine alfredo

Müller-Thurgau Estate
The expressive, tropical fruit is a fantastic contrast to spicy dishes, like Thai or Indian curries, shrimp tacos, or chèvre.

Tastings
Open to the public, year-round

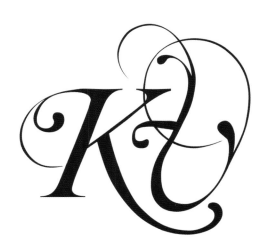

KRAMER
VINEYARDS

Lange Estate Winery and Vineyards

Dundee

While living and working with wine in Santa Barbara County in 1987, Don and Wendy Lange quickly ascertained that pinot noir was their highest priority as winemakers—and wine drinkers. When they stumbled upon two bottles of Oregon pinot noir—an Erath and an Eyrie—the die was cast. With Burgundy as their paradigm, the Langes were so impressed by the offerings from Oregon that the couple immediately began searching for vineyard land in the Willamette Valley. Within three months they had purchased their first 30 acres of land on the southeast slopes of the renowned Dundee Hills.

As is the Oregon way, neighbors pitched in to help the young winemakers get settled—Dick Erath called his friend Art Weber, of Weber Vineyards, to help get the Langes' press off the U-Haul truck with his old reliable John Deere tractor. David Lett, "Papa Pinot" from The Eyrie Vineyards, loaned the Langes his backup stemmer-crusher for their first three vintages. These early pioneers—the Benoits, the Letts, the Ponzis, the Sokol-Blossers—were all supportive in the collaborative effort to carve world-class wine out of the wilderness. Upon meeting Don and Wendy at a party, Mary Benoit, already a veteran at that point, said in her inimitable way that she hoped they were well-capitalized. They weren't, but that didn't seem to matter. Their first vintage, in 1987, was remarkable for two things: It was the earliest vintage on record, and the Langes became only the fourth producer of pinot gris in this new world.

Top: Founder and executive winemaker Don Lange is amused and intrigued by wine and music.

Bottom: Wendy Lange, CEO and founder, is both a tough businesswoman and the consummate caregiver to Minnie and her three other shelties, her chickens, stray cats, and her family.

Facing Page: Looking northward, Lange Estate Winery and Vineyards stands majestically against a backdrop of the Chehalem Valley and Mountains and, in the distance, the Oregon Coast Range.
Photographs by Andrèa Johnson

The Pinot Gris Reserve was quickly recognized as a benchmark bottling for one of the Willamette Valley's finest varietals. Over time the reputation for pinot gris, chardonnay, and of course pinot noir grew, and the case production went from 1,000 to just under 20,000. In 2004, Don's winemaking efforts were reinforced by the addition of son Jesse, who had first started making wine with his father when he was the ripe old age of five. Tasting freshly pressed pinot noir from the spout on the upright basket press, young Jesse proclaimed to his father, as the wine ran down his chin, that pinot noir is good. That tow-headed enophile is now the head winemaker and general manager at Lange Estate Winery and Vineyards.

Above: Pickers head into the Old Block at daybreak.
Photograph by Andréa Johnson

Right: Jesse Lange, winemaker and general manager, enjoys the scenery from the tasting terrace with his best friend Maggy. Jesse has crafted many 90-plus wines and has guided the winery to two Winery of the Year awards.
Photograph courtesy of Lange Estate Winery and Vineyards

Facing Page: Budbreak in the Old Block is all the more magical after a heavy rain.
Photograph by Don Lange

Previous Pages: The working family winery is comprised of a tasting room, a tasting terrace, a crush pad, offices, a barn, solar panels, and the original homestead.
Photograph by Andréa Johnson

At Lange Estate, the winemaking process encompasses thousands of decisions, some small and some large. One of the most important of these is the timing of harvest. As a varietal, pinot noir has a unique capacity to showcase the nuances of terroir. Because of this, the Langes pick more than 80 distinct blocks of pinot noir. The winemaking team is intently focused on picking grapes when the optimal balance is achieved between flavors, acids, and sugars. The Lange style of winemaking is defined by minimal, gentle handling of the grape and a non-interventionist approach in the cellar. There is no extended pre- or post-fermentation maceration, no dry ice, and minimal use of sulfur dioxide. The oak barrel regime is calibrated to subtly enhance the wines. Because the grapes are sourced from only the finest, proven sites, and intense focus is on balance, the Lange pinot noirs are well known for their aging potential.

The Lange family has worked with the finest family grape growers, some of them since the late 1980s. This group includes the Durant Vineyards, Freedom Hill Vineyard, and Yamhill Vineyards, all family-owned and all entering into their second generation of viticulturists and winemakers. These sites all include old vine blocks on distinct, and now legendary, terroirs. There is nothing in the wine business more important to the Lange family than the relationships with these friends and colleagues who are all committed to growing some of the finest wine grapes in the world.

Left: Don, Wendy, and Jesse relax outside the formal tasting room with some of their favorite things.
Photograph by Andréa Johnson

The acreage of the estate vineyards has grown as well, to include the acquisition of an additional 15 acres, the Mia Block, adjacent to the original property, and the 10-acre Redside Vineyard just to the east, bringing the total Dundee Hills acreage to 45. The winery and tasting room rest at a 750-foot elevation and overlook the northernmost part of the Willamette Valley, with unrivaled views of the Chehalem Range, the Cascades, Mount Jefferson, and Mount Hood. These vineyards and the Langes' winemaking philosophy earned Lange Estate 2012 Winery of the Year accolades from *Wine & Spirits Magazine* and Snooth.

Preserving the environment is a priority at Lange Estate. The winery received its LIVE certification in 2008 and continues to maintain the rigorous eco-friendly practices the organization requires for annual renewal. Certified Salmon-Safe, the winery uses a variety of sustainable practices. The Langes also encourage conservation of native species of salmonids by supporting the Native Fish Society and the Deschutes River Conservancy. Solar panels provide half of the electricity used at the winery and a water retention system is installed off the roof of the winery's barn. This recollected water is used for irrigation before any water is pulled from the well. A majority of the Lange Estate wines are bottled in ECO Series glass, a material that is produced from recycled glass in green energy-fueled facilities.

Establishing a philanthropic pedigree is also important. Education, the environment, health care, and music are priorities for the Lange family. Caldera Arts, Habitat for Humanity, Newberg Education Foundation, Salud!, and Sister's Folk Festival are just a few of the organizations that receive continual support and sponsorship from the winery.

Top: Don and Jesse enjoy a barrel sampling of Dundee Hills Pinot Noir.

Middle: The terrace boasts views of the valley and Mount Hood.

Bottom: Maggy loves Lange Estate Chardonnay.

Facing Page: When Jesse is not at the winery, he is fly-fishing one of Oregon's many blue-ribbon rivers. His steelhead rod and reel show the scale of a magnum of Lange Estate Three Hills Cuvée Pinot Noir.
Photographs by Andréa Johnson

WINE & FARE

Lange Estate Dundee Hills Pinot Noir
Pairs well with wood-smoked pork loin alongside fresh green beans.

Lange Estate Pinot Gris Reserve
Pairs elegantly with pork saltimbocca with polenta.

Lange Estate Reserve Pinot Noir
Serve alongside leg of lamb with a cherry-olive jus.

Lange Estate Willamette Valley Chardonnay
Pairs well with chicken, roasted bell pepper, and Fontina cheese panini.

Tastings
Open to the public daily

Laurel Ridge Winery

Carlton

The seeds of Laurel Ridge Winery were planted in 1960, when David Teppola continued his studies of philosophy and chemistry abroad in Europe. Fascinated with the Old World winemaking he saw there, David routed his interest in art and science into a lifelong passion for wine and winemaking. This passion came to fruition when David and his wife, Susan, planted what would become Laurel Ridge Winery's first vineyard in 1980.

Laurel Ridge Winery is truly a family affair. The couple's children, Kira and Maija, were born and raised here, on the 240-acre farm that David bought with his GI benefits. And, like our European progenitors, the idea was to fold wine into everyday activities—an enviable lifestyle to be sure. By keeping the process in a tight-knit group, Laurel Ridge Winery reaps the rewards of hard work and passion, passed along in bottle form.

Browse the Laurel Ridge Winery catalog, and you'll quickly be taken aback by the variety, especially in an area so well-known for pinot noir. At any time, you can find a wide selection rarely found in these parts—often 12 to 14 varieties on the menu, from port to riesling to one of the few méthode champenoise wines in the area. With whites, reds, dry, and sweet options, there's certainly something for everybody. Spread out in the garden, walk the picturesque perimeter, and soak in the beauty of your neighborhood winery as you sip some of Oregon's most noteworthy wines.

Top: The pet-friendly tasting room is also staffed by friendly people.

Bottom: The winery is widely known for its assortment of white and red wines, along with sparkling wine and port.

Facing Page: Designed to fit in with its agriculture neighbors, the building is camouflaged as a barn, while inside is a state-of-the-art winery and tasting room.
Photographs by Andréa Johnson

Left Coast Cellars

Rickreall

Left Coast Cellars is more than sustainably farmed vineyards and a solar-powered winery producing award-winning wines; a visit is a true experience for the senses. A winding road, amid flowers and vines, leads you through the natural agricultural landscape of the Willamette Valley, enhanced by a family's passion for gardening and winemaking.

Past the winery, situated atop a hill with picture-perfect views, the tasting room, accented in pine and painted antiques, is nestled among some of the oldest oak stands in the valley. There, or on the patio in fine weather, a warm welcome accompanies the excellent Left Coast wines—an extension of all those who contribute to their making. Here you discover an operation built on passion and a love of the land often taken for granted.

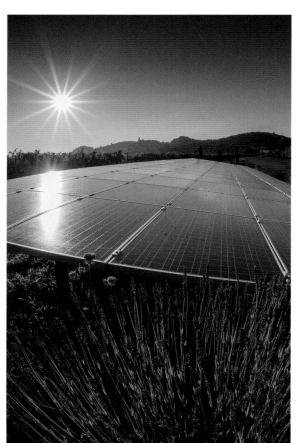

Left Coast Cellars is a 356-acre working farm, and its owners pride themselves on being stewards of the land. The outdoor Treehouse Pavilion is a tribute to this legacy; its central supports are fallen oaks, lost in the occasional storm, and the cherry crossbeams were found on property. The family's eldest son was married here. Fifty beehives are scattered across the land. The honey and Left Coast jams, such as Strawberry Pinot Noir, are available in the tasting room, along with locally sourced cheeses and charcuterie, hazelnuts, chocolate-dipped cherries, and produce-driven offerings from the estate's organic gardens. Estate chickens and ducks provide the eggs.

Chef Carolynn Andringa delights in creative pairings: estate-grown pears on a local blue cheese spread, arugula, and whole grain bread are perfection with a glass of Truffle Hill Chardonnay. Yes, there is truffle cultivation going on adjacent to this vineyard, which also produces an exquisite single-vineyard, designate all-Wädenswil clone pinot noir.

Top: Left Coast Cellars hired an iron worker and got an artist—the entrance gate is absolutely exquisite.

Bottom: The winery is powered by the sun.

Facing Page: The vineyards are tended with care. Right Bank and Latitude 45 are situated on the 45th parallel.
Photographs by Andréa Johnson

The dream of such a place grew from a Scandinavian heritage on matriarch Suzanne Larson's part, her great-grandparents having immigrated from Norway, homesteading and farming north of Seattle. Her world broadened during her junior year in Tuscany and then in a second year, when she lived in the Italian countryside, canning tomatoes, gathering mushrooms, curing olives and prosciutto, and stomping grapes to make a very modest first wine. The tasting room's farm-fresh market approach and Bee Sustainable refillable magnum program—a delicious, everyday table wine blend—draw from those memorable days. When newly married, a three-year stay in France brought weekends at the nurseries and at simple restaurants in the outskirts of Paris, providing direct inspiration for the tasting room and surrounding gardens. Burgundy was right there too, firmly planting the pinot bug in the young couple, which eventually brought them to establish Left Coast Cellars in one of the great pinot-growing regions of the world, Oregon's Willamette Valley.

The younger generation is equally involved in the operation. The eldest, Karleton, a Le Cordon Bleu graduate, has had his hand in the kitchen. Left-handed—three of five in the family are lefties!—daughter Cali, a landscape architect, shares her name with the winery's flagship wine, Cali's Cuvée. The 100-percent pinot noir is a blend of the fruit from

the estate's seven vineyards planted to pinot noir. The youngest, Taylor, works in the cellar and makes wine but is also studying toward an MBA in wine and spirits through the University of Bordeaux. He reports to and reveres his mentors: winemaker Joe Wright and viticulturist Luke McCollom. Founding winemaker Luke has been with the operation from the beginning, and now shoulders the weighty role of general manager.

What the land provides is evident here; even the label displays a Lewis and Clark map of the area. But of course what speaks most eloquently is that which is in the bottle. Observations of perfectly balanced acidity, seductive floral bouquets, finely grained tannins and, simply put, deliciousness, are often voiced about these wines.

Above: Feel the ocean breezes from the Van Duzer Corridor, where the Field of Dreams Vineyard is located.
Photograph by Andréa Johnson

Top Right: Left Coast's resident owl is among the migrating birds and birds of prey that balance animal life in the vineyards.
Photograph by Diane Stevenson

Bottom Right: Joe Wright is the winemaker.
Photograph by Andréa Johnson

Facing Page Top: A small part of the Left Coast family: Taylor Pfaff, Christina Aragon, Suzanne Larson, Luke McCollom, and Jenn Bell.
Photograph by Andréa Johnson

Facing Page Bottom: Fruit trees have been added to the historic orchards now under vine, dating to the pioneers who settled Oregon.
Photograph by Diane Stevenson

Recognitions abound not only for Left Coast's pinot noirs, but also for its chardonnays, pinot blanc, pinot gris, and the instantly sold-out white pinot. The 2012 Rosé of Pinot Noir received the top accolade in a tasting of nearly 100 northwest rosés; the 2011 Cali's Cuvée was honored with a double gold in the 2013 Oregon Wine Awards; and the 2012 vintage of Cali's was given a 92 rating by *Wine & Spirits Magazine*. Suzanne is catching up with her daughter: The 2010 barrel select, Suzanne's Estate Reserve, like the single-vineyard designate pinot noir, Latitude 45, both received scores of 92 from *Wine Spectator*.

At Left Coast Cellars, you eat estate, drink estate, and discover a world of unforgettable experiences. This is a magical place, nurtured with care and dedicated to its art, handcrafting the best that can come from this land. End your visit on the hiking trails and linger in one of Cali's stump gardens, seasonally and happily open to guests. This, a glass of wine, a bowl of local berries, a plate of heirloom tomatoes from the gardens, and a bunch of flowers to take home with you is life at Left Coast Cellars. The wine and food pairing suggestions are among those changing seasonally and served in the tasting room daily.

Above: Cali's Cuvée Pinot Noir was named for the daughter of the family. Cali Pfaff.

Left: Summertime is perfect on the tasting room patio.

Facing Page: Visits are characterized by warm welcomes and reluctant goodbyes.
Photographs by Andréa Johnson

WINE & FARE

Truffle Hill Chardonnay
(100% chardonnay)
Pair with potato-corn chowder with plenty of Italian parsley
and cayenne pepper.

Cali's Cuvée
(100% pinot noir)
Pair with roasted grapes with white sweet onion and olive oil
on toasted bruschetta.

Rosé of Pinot Noir
(100% pinot noir)
Pair with watermelon gazpacho with green bell peppers, vine-ripened
tomatoes, and fresh garlic.

Tastings
Open to the public, year-round

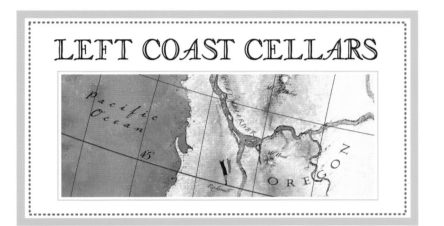

Lemelson Vineyards

Carlton

Although he did not realize it at the time, Eric Lemelson found his niche in the Oregon wine business by listening to his muse, following his intuition, and choosing the paths that appeared before him. The eldest son of noted independent inventor Jerome Lemelson, Eric has the iconoclastic and entrepreneurial spirit that embodies Oregon wine country in his blood. When he decided to attend Portland's Reed College in 1979, Eric didn't have a sense of place, but he quickly developed a strong awareness of Oregon's uniqueness after he arrived. His career path took several turns after college, including time devoted to politics, earning a degree in environmental law from Lewis & Clark, and several years as the law school's director of a research center on western water law. While in law school, early in 1990, he saw an ad in the local newspaper for a hillside farm on the eastern edge of Oregon wine country, and wound up as a late arrival in the back-to-the-land movement.

Eric knew that the property he purchased had areas suitable for wine grapes. In the mid-1990s he discovered, and was inspired by, several benchmark examples of Oregon pinot noir. After enjoying their bottled inspiration, he contacted the winemakers and began a quest to learn as much as he could about viticulture. With the knowledge he gained from extensive research, he planted two acres of pinot noir and pinot gris as a hobby farm, and left his law career within a few years to jump into the wine business with both feet. Today the winery consistently ranks among the best producers in the Pacific Northwest.

Top: Proprietor Eric Lemelson carries on his family's legacy of creativity and ingenuity.

Bottom Left & Facing Page: Lemelson has farmed organically since the beginning, embracing the mantra that what's good for the vineyards and wine is also good for the community.
Photographs by Andréa Johnson

Eric's background in environmental law fuels the Lemelson philosophy of environmentally conscious winemaking. His commitment to sustainability is complemented by winemaker Anthony King's interest and research into the effects that vineyard practices have on pinot noir's color and tannin. Together they craft unique pinot noirs using innovative winemaking technology, only where appropriate, and a gentle hand along every step of the way.

The focus on sustainability is part of Eric's long-term philosophy, and hence forms a core part of the values at Lemelson. The winery has a 50-kilowatt solar panel array that generates about a third of the power used annually, and all winery employees are offered substantial incentives to drive highly fuel-efficient cars. Lemelson Vineyards was also one of the founding members of the Oregon wine industry's Carbon Neutral Challenge in 2006, designed to reduce the industry's impact on climate change. Eric also runs a small Oregon-based charitable foundation

that focuses on climate change adaptation funding in Bhutan, a small but important country in the Himalayas seeing major impacts from a warming world.

The multilevel gravity-flow winery not only features energy-conserving underground barrel storage, but also employs a unique, 14-foot-tall mobile sorting platform. The device, which looks like a huge metal spider, allows the winemakers to selectively position a de-stemmer over any fermentation vessel in the main room of the winery. The platform, known affectionately by the Lemelson team as the "Enterprise," assists the winemaking team to more accurately sort and remove underripe and moldy grape clusters before they enter the stainless steel fermentation tanks.

Above & Right: Cool-climate varietals benefit from sophisticated gravity-flow processing. The winery has an impressive 12,000-case capacity.

Facing Page Bottom: Winemaker Anthony King has a longstanding passion for pinot noir.
Photographs by Andréa Johnson

The seven distinct vineyard sites reflect the variation in western Oregon's climate, soils, and aspects. In cooler years, lower elevation sites usually produce the best wines, while in warmer years, high elevation sites such as Chestnut Hill produce elegant, velvety pinot noirs and several noteworthy white wines as well. The Lemelson portfolio includes a number of distinctive bottlings of single-vineyard and blended pinot noirs, as well as chardonnay, dry riesling, and pinot gris.

Visitors are invited to visit the winery and explore the facility and its beautiful, welcoming setting. Constructed as much as possible from locally sourced, certified building materials from regional vendors and artisans, the winery emerges seamlessly from the hillside topography.

Above, Left & Facing Page: Lemelson's commitment to sustainability begins in the vineyards and extends to every facet of the operations. Constructed with responsibly harvested wood and filled with natural light, the winery is a beautiful place to celebrate.
Photographs by Andréa Johnson

WINE & FARE

Tikka's Run Pinot Gris
Serve alongside baked salmon, stuffed mussels, or ginger-spiced shrimp.

Dry Riesling
Perfect with grilled snapper with lime-tomatillo sauce, Thai green curry, or ceviche.

Theas Selection Pinot Noir
Pairs well with braised pork chops, chanterelle mushroom risotto, and Comte cheese.

Jerome Reserve Pinot Noir
Serve alongside roast duck, lamb with root vegetables, or triple cream cheese.

Tastings
Open to the public, Thursday through Monday

LEMELSON
VINEYARDS

Maysara Winery

McMinnville

"Whatever is in the heart will come up to the tongue—with drunkenness comes the truth."
Persian Proverb

Historically, wine was considered to be of sacred nature in the ancient Persian culture or customs. In order to keep the origin of the Momtazi family and history of wine, it was important that the naming of the winery reflected their roots. Maysara Winery is derived from the archaic words may and sara, translating as "House of Wine."

On April 1, 1997, Moe and Flora Momtazi, purchased 496 acres of uncultivated, abandoned wheat farm and set about to create a winery that represented the Persian wine heritage. Over the next few years with additions of purchasing neighboring properties brought the total acreage to 532 acres. The first year at the Momtazi estate was crucial, as the preparation of the land was the most important concern to protect the integrity of the estate grafted vines of pinot gris, pinot blanc, gewürztraminer, Muscat, Pommard, and Dijon 113, 114, 115, 667 and 777. Since the beginning, the Momtazis knew the importance of keeping the land and resources on the property unfertilized to preserve the natural integrity of the Momtazi vineyard. Luckily, the estate had more than nine soil types suited for the growing of grapes, lush forestry, streams of fresh pure water and a variety of fruits that thrived growing naturally.

Staying true to the family's Persian heritage, Maysara Winery manifests a connection to the historical winegrowing region that once existed in Iran. In 2001, *Wine Spectator* published Matthew DeBord's, "Wine Artifacts from Ancient Iran" that examined Bronze Age ceramics to testify to the deep cultural roots of ancient Iran's love of wine. The DNA tested from the artifacts that were found in Feerooz Abad, Iran, trace residue of zinfandel 7,500 years ago.

Top: Tasting room entrance.
Photograph by Naseem Momtazi

Bottom: The Momtazi family Hanna, Tahmiene, Moe, Naseem, and Flora.
Photograph by Andréa Johnson

Facing Page: Reflection of Momtazi Vineyard onto the reservoir.
Photograph by Andréa Johnson

Over the recent years, Maysara Winery has become a true family affair. Moe, the patriarch of the family designates his time to farming his renowned vineyard. Flora handles not only the financial portion of the business, but is heavily involved in the landscaping of the winery. All three daughters have joined forces upon graduating college. The eldest, Tahmiene, joined the team in 2007, becoming one of the youngest head female winemakers in the United States at age 24. Naseem, the middle daughter, took over international and national sales in 2009, while the youngest, Hanna began focusing on marketing of the brand in 2013. The first vintage for Maysara Winery was produced in 2001, and fittingly, the lineup of wines consisted of Persian terms to identify each label: Arsheen Pinot Gris, Autees Pinot Blanc, Roseena Rosé, Jamsheed Pinot Noir, Cyrus Pinot Noir, Delara Pinot Noir, and Mitra Pinot Noir. The backs of all labels describe the namesake.

As a Demeter Certified Biodynamic producer, Maysara Winery set out to create one of the largest biodynamic ecosystems to preserve the land as a whole in Oregon. Keeping the land's forestry and native habitat intact prevents the depletion of nutrients throughout the property. The trees preserve the natural habitat for the birds and other animals; fruit trees and flowers attract beneficial insects that promote value to plants. Momtazi Vineyard cultivates more than 10 plants, including stinging nettle, chamomile, horsetail, yarrow, and dandelions; the crew then prepares tea-like sprays that are 100-percent consumable for personal intake that is used throughout the vines to naturally fight against diseases or help avoid malnutrition. These biodynamic practices date back centuries before conventional, convenient, cost-cutting farming popularized the use of fertilizers and chemicals. The integrity of the Momtazi land is showcased not only in Maysara estate wines, but also to the many premium producers who bottle Momtazi vineyard designated wines. In a short amount of time, Maysara wines have received a vast amount of recognition to attest to their quality. The winery was ranked number 14 of *Wine Spectator's* 2012 Top 100 Wines.

Top: View of Mount Hood from the hilltop.
Photograph by Moe Momtazi

Middle: Winter wonderland.
Photograph by Moe Momtazi

Bottom: Vineyard crew working during harvest.
Photograph by Andrèa Johnson

Facing Page: Higher elevation of Momtazi Vineyard.
Photograph by Moe Momtazi

In 2008, the winery broke ground for the development of what originally was intended to be a pole barn, which evolved into the new winery production and tasting room. Ninety five-percent of the material used to build the structure was from the land and or of recycled products—a fact that always draws fascination. A prime example: The interior walls are lined with 1,100 used barrels. The winery, approximately 42,000 square feet, is held up by 18 Douglas fir columns that rise 35 feet tall. Moe, a civil engineer by trade, designed and engineered the building alongside his own team to create his legacy of a building. After years of construction, the first use of the facility was for the 2013 vintage. In 2014, Maysara Winery's building was recognized in *Brides Magazine* as one of the best venues in America on the west coast.

Above: Sunrise and foggy hills at sunrise.
Photograph by Andréa Johnson

Left: Flora and Moe Momtazi
Photograph by Andréa Johnson

Facing Page: View of the first 13 acres planted in 1998.
Photograph by Moe Momtazi

Autees Pinot Blanc
(100% pinot blanc)
Pair with firmer cheese, fresh fruit, and subtly herbed seafood.

Three Degrees Pinot Noir
(100% pinot noir)
Pair with curries, spetzatinas, and rich stews.

Roseena Rosé Pinot Noir
(100% pinot noir)
Pair with warm baker's spice, clean fruit, and sweet peppers.

Tastings:
Open to the public daily, May through October,
and Monday through Saturday November through April

McMenamins
Edgefield Winery

Troutdale

Historic McMenamins Edgefield is a truly remarkable destination. Built in 1911 as the Multnomah County Poor Farm just outside of Portland, its 74 acres now include a 100-room hotel, winery and wine tasting room, vineyards, distillery, brewery, two restaurants, seven bars, concert venue, golf course, spa and soaking pool, gardens, and gift shop. It is also listed on the National Register of Historic Places.

Brothers Mike and Brian McMenamin, who were instrumental in creating Oregon's first post-Prohibition brewpubs, transformed what was once an overgrown and abandoned poor farm into a gemstone of their family of neighborhood pubs and entertaining destinations. Work began in 1990 with the creation of the winery and the planting of vineyards and extensive gardens. The restoration progressed quickly to include the onsite 32-barrel brew house, the pub, Black Rabbit Restaurant, the distillery, and myriad small bars and niches to explore. Today Edgefield Winery crushes 350 tons of grapes annually to produce a range of bottled and draft wine for the 57 McMenamins pubs throughout Oregon and Washington. In addition to producing and directly distributing an average of 25,000 cases of wine each year, the winery also creates the popular Edgefield draft hard apple cider, keeping the winery humming with its 30,000 gallons of production.

The Edgefield Winery tasting room is nestled in a red brick cellar of the historic Edgefield Manor; a cool and dark, yet inviting, space where guests, wine tanks, barrels, and nightly musical entertainment form a lively, interactive, and intimate atmosphere. Choose from a selection of red, white, rosé, dessert, and sparkling wines available for purchase by the glass, bottle, or case. Visitors are welcome to enjoy wine over candlelight at night, or to step outside and walk with wine in hand to explore the expansive, scenic property.

Top: The Edgefield Tasting Room is open every day, with free live music nightly.
Photograph by Andréa Johnson

Bottom: All hands are on deck at crush time, just outside the Edgefield Winery.
Photograph courtesy of McMenamins Edgefield Winery

Facing Page: Edgefield's hotel is nestled adjacent to one of the vineyards on the expansive property.
Photograph courtesy of McMenamins Edgefield Winery

Edgefield Winery continues to produce cool-climate varieties like pinot gris, pinot noir, and riesling, working with a select handful of Willamette Valley and Southern Oregon growers to produce aromatic whites and delicate reds, along with sparkling and blush wines. As the winery grew, fruit from Columbia Gorge and Columbia Valley vineyards allowed the winemakers to craft red wines of larger stature. When Edgefield Distillery opened in 1998, McMenamins winemakers and distillers collaborated to create high-proof brandy for a breadth of fortified port-style wines.

"Our extensive variety of wines and the wide range of varietals and growing climate sets Edgefield Winery apart," says winemaker Davis Palmer, who works with director of winery and distillery operations Clark McCool. "We showcase the unique expression and varietal character from each grape, while exploring the interplay between varietals in larger blends such as our flagship Black Rabbit Red, Cuvée de l'Abri Rouge, and White Rabbit."

Food and wine pairings are featured at special events throughout the year, such as the Celebration of Syrah every April at Edgefield. Syrah aficionados can sample more than 50 syrah wines from McMenamins and winemakers around the world.

At Edgefield, life is about handcrafting wine, spirits, and beer, and bringing people together in eclectic pubs, bars, restaurants, and lush outdoor settings.

Top: A visit to Edgefield begins where the beauty and creative whimsy of the landscaping, artwork, and history lift the spirits. In the tasting room, wine flights offer an exploration of Edgefield Winery's diverse selection.
Photograph courtesy of McMenamins Edgefield Winery

Middle: Visitors are encouraged to roam around the Edgefield property, beverage in hand.
Photograph courtesy of McMenamins Edgefield Winery

Bottom: Wine is aged in barrels onsite, including barrels from the Edgefield Distillery.
Photograph by Andréa Johnson

Facing Page: McMenamins Edgefield is a 25-minute drive from downtown Portland, and is open daily to welcome visitors for an experience like no other.
Photograph courtesy of McMenamins Edgefield Winery

Syrah
Delicious with barbecue beef spare ribs, grilled tuna steaks, strongly flavored sausages, and aged cheeses.

Black Rabbit Red
A great accompaniment to stroganoff, pot roast, hamburgers, cow's milk cheeses, and hearty meals with root vegetables, mushrooms, and spices.

Fireside Zinfandel
Pair with chocolate-based desserts, ice cream, cookies, fudge, and roasted nuts.

Tastings
Open to the public daily

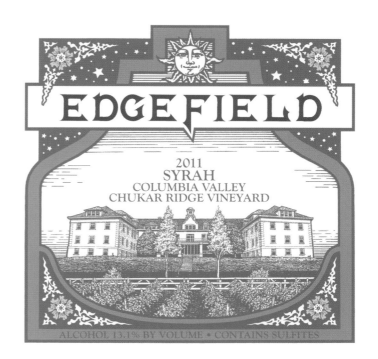

Methven Family Vineyards
Dayton

For Dr. Allen Methven, the pathway to the vineyards was forged through his dental practice—and during late nights of friendly poker games at his home. Some of his patients, such as Don Byers, Dick Erath, and Myron Redford, were among the original forefathers in Oregon's burgeoning wine industry. Whether in the dental chair or dealing the cards, they were encouraging Allen and his wife, Jill, to plant grapes and join the vintner club in Oregon.

It took more than a year of convincing, but Allen and Jill made the decision to move forward and purchased a perfect site to plant their vineyard, featuring more than 100-acres. In the beginning they planted 25 acres, and six years later, they planted another eight acres and built a winery on the property.

Under the meticulous eye of winemaker Chris Lubberstedt, Methven Family Vineyards exclusively produces estate varietals of chardonnay, gamay noir, pinot gris, pinot noir, and riesling in small lots, each hand-selected for quality and consistency. The winery also sells its premium grapes to vintners in Oregon and has a custom crush program to craft signature wines by request.

But it's not only the integrity of their award-winning wines that's distinctive. One of the most rewarding aspects for Jill and Allen is welcoming guests to the vineyards. Visitors are greeted with a unique and congenial experience at the tasting room, which is beautifully situated amid the vines. With a commercial kitchen onsite, artful, chef-prepared food and wine pairings are frequently on the menu as well.

Top: Owners Jill and Allen Methven at the entrance to their tasting room.

Bottom: View of the Methven's House Block vineyard site.

Facing Page: Looking down from the Methvens' home onto the vineyard and the winery in the background.
Photographs by Andréa Johnson

For longer stays, the Estate Villa is a charming, Tuscan-inspired bed-and-breakfast that overlooks the property's rolling countryside, along with remarkable views of Mount Hood and the Cascades. The picturesque location is also a natural fit for weddings and other special events. An expert team accommodates every whim, delighting with handcrafted and customized affairs that are truly unforgettable.

For Allen, who splits his time between the vines and his dentistry practice in Dundee, it's all about diversification. He and Jill also dabble in beekeeping and cultivating blueberries at their vineyards. But winemaking is their true labor of love, and the sharing of their premier wine with others is the biggest reward, whether it's on the property or outside of Oregon.

They have so far chosen to distribute the product in locations where they have personal ties, including Alaska, California, Florida, Hawaii, Illinois, Louisiana, Michigan, New York, Tennessee, Texas, and Washington. In fact, one of their most significant memories—and proudest moments— was discovering that their favorite hotel in the world, the Grand Hotel on Mackinac Island, Michigan, featured Methven Family Vineyards' pinot gris on the wine list.

Top: Methven Family Vineyards' sign at the entrance to the winery.

Bottom: Winemaker Chris Lubberstedt in the winery.

Facing Page: View of the vineyard and bocce ball court.
Photographs by Andréa Johnson

WINE & FARE

Citizen's Cuvée Pinot Noir
Beautiful alongside smoked salmon or gravlax.

Gamay Noir
The ideal accompaniment to roasted turkey and gravy.

Estate Cuvée Pinot Noir
Pairs robustly with spaghetti Bolognese.

Riesling
Perfect with pear compote.

Pinot Gris
Pairs well with salmon, mango salsa, and savory pork chops with grilled peaches.

Tastings
Open to the public daily

Noble Estate
Vineyard and Winery

Eugene

Surrounded by Noble firs, Noble Estate Vineyard and Winery didn't have to look far for its name. As luck would have it for owner and winemaker Mark Jurasevich, the southern Willamette Valley location wasn't just perfect for trees, it was also ideal for growing grapes with its prime Bellpine and Jory soils. Now the land is lush with vines.

Mark had one goal in mind when he planted his first grapes in 1999: to make a fine pinot noir for his wife, Marie. His goal quickly became a passion, and he soon added chardonnay, Muscat, and riesling to the 20-acre vineyard. From pruning and sorting to de-stemming, pressing, and bottling, everything is done by hand at the family-owned Noble Estate. They nurture the grapes, cluster by cluster, for maximum exposure to the richest soil and sunlight. "The quality and character of the grapes determines the quality and character of the wine," says Mark, whose winemaking philosophy combines modern techniques with sustainable farming.

With such handcrafted care, it's no surprise that Noble Estate's wines have consistently been award winners. The Pinot Noir Vineyard Select, which pairs beautifully with grilled seafood, as well as the Semi-Sparkling Muscat—a perfect accompaniment to fresh fruit tarts—are two of the most consistently honored. Visitors to the winery can enjoy a robust list, including cabernet sauvignon, gewürztraminer, merlot, sauvignon blanc, syrah, and viognier. The view is worth savoring as well. Overlooking the Pacific Coast mountain range, the Eugene Tasting Room is surrounded by the vineyards and beautiful old-growth firs. About 80 miles from the property is Noble Estate's second tasting room in Yachats, "the gem of the Oregon coast."

Top: Winemaker Mark Jurasevich sampling a new vintage of Noble Estate's award-winning Muscat.

Bottom: Noble Estate pinot noir vineyards in the early morning after fall harvest.

Facing Page: Noble Estate was started in 1999. The name comes from the Noble fir tree.
Photographs by Andréa Johnson

Oak Knoll Winery

Hillsboro

Breaking ground is the inevitable seed of winemaking, and Oak Knoll Winery's longevity and consistency has certainly been groundbreaking. The winery's story began in 1970, when the Vuylsteke family became early pioneers of the Oregon wine industry by founding the first winery in Washington County. At that time, there were only a few vineyards and a handful of wineries in all of Oregon.

By 2003, the winery had its second generation of family maintaining a passionate commitment. The goal: to re-establish the winery as a historical treasure moving into modern winemaking while maintaining a sense of the past. Today a team of six runs the whole operation. Close to downtown Portland, the family draws some of the most fascinating fruit from a selection of vineyards within a 10-mile radius of the winery—with so many microclimates, Oak Knoll manages to bring out the true expressions of pinot noir, pinot gris, and a multitude of dessert wines. The American Niagara, for instance, is one of Oak Knoll's longest-running wines, and certainly one of its most popular. Though many of Oak Knoll's bottles are 100-percent true varietals, the occasional blend rears its head in the Toasted Cow series. Or grab a bottle of Deviant Sweet Red Revolution, a wine that is plotting a coup against the tyranny of wine snobbery.

Oak Knoll Winery's endurance is made possible in part by the family's determination to have fun with the lifestyle. The winery's place in the community is an indicator. As the official wine of the Portland Rose Festival and the host of a summer concert series, Oak Knoll Winery has managed to blend great wine with a great experience.

Top: The winery building was constructed in the early 1970s with Oregon cedar from a nearby property.

Middle: Winery dog Lucee is always waiting for an opportunity to sneak a sip.

Bottom: Winemaker and family cousin Jeff Herinckx inspects incoming fruit quality, just as he has for the past 30 years.

Facing Page: Oak Knoll's Red Hill Vineyard Pinot Noir.
Photographs by Andréa Johnson

Patton Valley Vineyard

Gaston

Patton Valley Vineyard's beginnings date back to the early 1980s, when business school classmates Dave Chen and Monte Pitt dreamed of turning their passion for wine into a business. A decade later, after many conversations and many more bottles of pinot noir, they took the plunge and, in 1995, purchased 72 acres in Oregon's Willamette Valley. What started as a dream between friends became a reality with the initial 10 acres planted in 1997.

Great wine begins in the vineyard; this age-old adage is the guiding principle at Patton Valley. Located in the northern reaches of the Willamette Valley, the vineyard benefits from exposures to the east, the south, and over a hilltop to the west, enabling the production of distinctly different wines from one vineyard. To showcase the true nature of the vineyard, Patton Valley employs low-impact winemaking techniques and sustainable farming practices, protecting the integrity of the wine and the vineyard. Beyond its impact on the wine, the people at Patton Valley strive to take sustainability one step further, using their land to increase the natural biodiversity of their property by housing bees, reintroducing native plants, and installing raptor posts and bird boxes throughout the vineyard.

Owners Dave, Monte, and Sherie are joined by Napa Valley native Derek Einberger, who serves as winemaker and vineyard manager. Derek brings his experience gained in Italy, Napa, and other parts of the Willamette Valley to Patton Valley Vineyard, where he crafts exceptional, terroir-focused wine. Tasting room hours are 11am-5pm, Thursday through Monday.

Top: Monte Pitt, Sherie Pitt, and Dave Chen are the winery's owners.
Photograph by Andréa Johnson

Middle: Sunrise is spectacular at Patton Valley Vineyard.
Photograph by Andréa Johnson

Bottom: Winemaker Derek Einberger tastes wine during fermentation.
Photograph by Andréa Johnson

Facing Page: The vineyard and winery are ideally located in the Wallamette Valley.
Photograph courtesy of Skyris Imaging and Patton Valley Vineyard

Penner-Ash Wine Cellars
Newberg

Nestled into the hillside overlooking the Chehalem Valley, Penner-Ash Wine Cellars stands as an accessible example of thoughtful winemaking. There is no pretense in the tasting room and no secret to the winemaking process at Penner-Ash, where the owners and staff connect with wine enthusiasts on a personal level. Careful tending of the vines, precise and experienced winemaking, education, and community involvement set the winery apart and illustrate why Oregon is different from other winemaking regions in the world.

In 1998, owners Lynn and Ron Penner-Ash decided to take their destiny into their own hands. The challenge of owning a business was the perfect pairing of their love of wine and entrepreneurial spirit. They established Penner-Ash Wine Cellars with sustainability and transparency as their hallmarks. After completing her enology and viticulture degree at UC Davis, Lynn began her career at Domaine Chandon and Stag's Leap Wine Cellars before joining the Oregon wine industry with Rex Hill Winery in 1988. There she served as president and winemaker before leaving to pursue her dreams with Ron to focus on Penner-Ash Wine Cellars.

Ron's goals mirrored those of his wife; after 20 years in education, he was prepared to tackle the challenges and rewards of owning a winery. The patience learned from his career as a teacher continues to pay off in the day-to-day operations at Penner-Ash. It is the unpredictability of nature and the science behind the winemaking process that inspires the pair to create distinctive wines year after year.

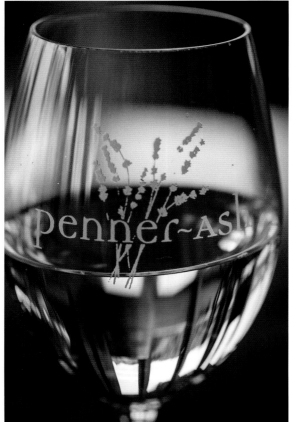

Top: The Estate Vineyard is planted to 100-percent pinot noir on both volcanic and marine sedimentary soils.
Photograph courtesy of Penner-Ash Wine Cellars

Bottom: Each Penner-Ash glass features the logo and a sun print of a botanical found on the estate property.
Photograph by Andréa Johnson

Facing Page: The LIVE certified, three-level gravity-flow winery is located on the northern edge of the Yamhill-Carlton AVA.
Photograph by Andréa Johnson

The winery's Estate Vineyard benefits from both sedimentary and volcanic soils producing complexity, nuance, and fruit forward characteristics. Beautifully textured, balanced, and well-crafted, the Penner-Ash Pinot Noir consistently ranks among the best of Oregon wines and has garnered praise from both Robert Parker Jr. and Steve Tanzer. In 2013, *Wine & Spirits Magazine* named Penner-Ash Wine Cellars as one of the most popular wines served in restaurants.

Above: Ron and Lynn Penner-Ash sample a tank of fermenting pinot noir.

Right: Experimenting with small-lot pinot noir fermentors that use oak barrels.

Facing Page Top & Bottom Left: The Estate Vineyard is divided into blocks based on soils and clonal selection. Clones include Pommard and Dijon clones 114, 115, 777, and 667.

Facing Page Bottom Right: Empty two-ton open-top stainless steel fermentors line the second level of the winery.
Photographs by Andréa Johnson

Lynn and Ron have made it their goal to take the mystery out of winemaking. As evidence of this, the tasting room is the perfect place for viewing all three floors of the winery's production areas. Stainless steel fermentation tanks and barrel cellars are easily viewed while sipping on sustainably grown wines. To insure diversity in fruit sources, Penner-Ash also manages and produces wine from numerous prestigious vineyards in the North Willamette Valley and southern Oregon, including Bella Vida Vineyard, Hyland Vineyard, and Shea Vineyard. For white wine lovers, the Penner-Ash Viognier boasts spirited aromatics of orange blossoms, honeysuckle, and peach. A wine with a luxurious mouthfeel, notes of bright stone fruit and lemon custard finish the viognier, giving it an acidity that tastes like summer.

The winery is heavily involved in the community. In addition to the industry's open house tasting days on Memorial Day weekend and Thanksgiving weekend, the winery hosts numerous chef and winemaker dinners, nonprofit fundraisers, and educational wine seminars. Penner-Ash's Summer Benefit Music Series supports local nonprofit organizations and provides a stunning backdrop to guest chefs and music lovers. Each year the winery participates in Salud!, a barrel auction in support of health care for vineyard workers and their families. The ideals of family, sustainability, and transparency are truly behind every bottle of Penner-Ash wine.

Top: The northwest-inspired Fireside Room is perfect for sipping wine next to the fireplace.

Middle: The sun rises over the expansive gardens of Penner-Ash, including the staff's year-round vegetable garden.

Bottom: Lynn tastes barrel samples of the Estate Vineyard-designated pinot noir

Facing Page: Sunset on the terrace greets guests with expansive views of Mount Hood and the Chehalem Valley.
Photographs by Andréa Johnson

Penner-Ash Willamette Valley Pinot Noir
Pair with salt-roasted Prairie Creek beet borscht with whipped
goat cheese and caraway.

Penner-Ash Hyland Vineyard Pinot Noir
Serve with panko-baked cod with arugula purée.

Penner-Ash Riesling
Perfect alongside lemongrass-barbecued pork and fresh green salad.

Penner-Ash Viognier
Pairs elegantly with spice-rubbed poultry and roasted root vegetables.

Tastings
Open to the public daily, tours by appointment

Plum Hill Vineyards

Gaston

Fate, jest, and passion are the three most important ingredients at Gaston's Plum Hill Vineyards, a surprise dream come true for owners RJ and Juanita Lint. As they enjoyed corporate management careers in California, RJ and Juanita lived in the shadow of Napa Valley, where they fostered a love and appreciation of wine. When the couple moved to Oregon in 1999, it's no surprise that winemaking was prominent on their radar.

After volunteering at local wineries for about five years—RJ also took winemaking classes at various institutions—the Lints planted a small vineyard beside their home, situated on a hill with lovely views of Forest Grove and Verboort. They even gave their vines whimsical monikers, such as "The Grape Gatsby" and "Sir Wineston Churchill." Their initial planting's success led to the 2007 purchase of a former dairy farm five miles from their home. After clearing away 151 Christmas tree stumps and more blackberry vines than they care to remember, their winery was in full force. RJ and Juanita say that the timing just seemed right.

Right indeed, as their first vineyard, known as Forest Grove, and the newer Gaston site offer visitors a variety of succulent pinots in addition to other wines. Visitors don't just taste wine when they visit Plum Hill, they linger in the vineyard's hospitality and beauty. RJ or Juanita are always present, and there's a picnic area with breathtaking views of Mount St. Helens and Mount Adams—not to mention a 120-foot-long dog run for furry friends. The Lints pour their heart and soul into every glass of wine because, for them, owning a winery is a dream they feel fortunate to experience and share.

Top: A fountain graces the front door of the tasting room, which is adjacent to the 100-year-old barn.

Bottom: Plum Hill's Winemaker's Barrel Select Pinot Noir has a waxed top.

Facing Page: The view of one of the vineyard blocks can be enjoyed from the back patio.
Photographs by Andréa Johnson

RoxyAnn Winery

Medford

As one of southern Oregon's oldest orchards, the Hillcrest property that stretches along the base of the slopes of Roxy Ann Peak is now the home of award-winning RoxyAnn Winery. When Reginald Parsons purchased the property in 1898, the Hillcrest Orchard produced prolific crops of pears. In subsequent years, the Parsons family built a large residence on the land, which is now included on the National Register of Historic Places. The family-owned business thrived, weathering the Great Depression and both World Wars, to emerge triumphant. But it isn't just pears that come from the volcanic and sedimentary soils of the Hillcrest property.

In 1997, Reginald's grandson Jack Day oversaw the planting of 20 acres along the southwest slopes of Roxy Ann Peak with wine grapes. There the shallow, limestone-clay soils and spectacular southern exposure mimic the conditions of Bordeaux, France. The first harvest of RoxyAnn wine was celebrated in 2001 with 150 cases of a proprietary bottling of red claret: a blend of cabernet sauvignon and merlot. It sold out within two weeks. With a strong commitment to conservation, the family-owned property produces primarily Bordeaux and Rhône-style grapes on 65 acres from its shallow soils. The eco-conscious winery also produces nearly 15,000 cases of wine, including cabernet Franc, cabernet sauvignon, chardonnay, claret, pinot gris, pinot noir, merlot, sauvignon blanc, syrah, tempranillo, and viognier under the direction of veteran winemaker John Quinones. With a focus on tried-and-true varietals, John and his team continue to explore new ways to showcase the distinctive terroir of the RoxyAnn vineyards.

Top: RoxyAnn Winery's tasting room is located in a historic barn built in 1918 and repurposed in 2003 for the tasting room.

Middle: The winery is led by winemaker John Quinones, general manager Chad Day, and proprietor Jack Day.

Bottom: RoxyAnn Winery primarily grows Bordeaux and Rhône-style grapes on 65 acres of shallow, clay soils.

Facing Page: Looking south through the Rogue Valley with RoxyAnn Winery's vineyard and Hillcrest Orchard's pear orchards in the foreground. The property has been owned and operated by Reginald Parsons and his descendants since 1908.
Photographs by Andréa Johnson

Saffron Fields Vineyard

Yamhill

Oregon wine country's green, sloping vineyards and strong sense of community captured the hearts of wine enthusiasts Dr. Angela Summers and Sanjeev Lahoti. During a tour of the Willamette Valley in 2003, Angela and Sanjeev saw their future in the site they later named Saffron Fields Vineyard. While the Houston, Texas, residents wanted to research their options to the fullest before settling on a property to purchase, it was the very first property they viewed, and simply felt right. The couple decided to go with their hearts and purchased the property on a hill in the Yamhill-Carlton AVA.

Traveling back and forth between Oregon and Texas, Angela and Sanjeev built a small house on the property and began to plant the vineyard. The first 10 acres of pinot noir were planted in 2007, and two years later the couple celebrated Saffron Fields Vineyard's first harvest. Although their initial intent was to only grow grapes for other wineries, one barrel tasting changed everything. With that one sample, they knew they had something special. The couple asked Tony Rynders to make 50 cases of pinot noir in 2010, officially launching the vineyard into the Oregon wine industry.

Top: Vines turn a brilliant golden saffron color in the fall, giving the vineyard its name.

Bottom: The old-block pinot noir is an important part of the property.

Facing Page: Pinot noir vines planted on the hilltop stretch to the clouds.
Photographs by Andréa Johnson

Tony began his career working in California wineries, but like so many before him quickly fell in love with the vineyards of the Pacific Northwest. After stints with Argyle Winery in Oregon and The Hogue Cellars in Washington, Tony became the head winemaker at Domaine Serene, where he held the position for 10 years. During his time with Domaine Serene, he received more 90-plus scores from *Wine Spectator Magazine* than any other winemaker during the same period of time. Angela and Sanjeev began collaborating with Tony after he had established his own consulting and premium crush service companies.

Above: The tasting room features a contemporary art collection and a Japanese garden.

Right: Angela Summers and Sanjeev Lahoti adore their dogs, Lily and Iris.

Facing Page: Catalan sculptor Jaume Plensa's "Tale Teller II" overlooks the Japanese garden designed by Hoichi Kurisu.
Photographs by Andréa Johnson

Tony took the pinot noir grapes from the fine soils of Saffron Fields Vineyard and produced an alluring wine: the Yamhill-Carlton Pinot Noir. The wine gives aromas of fresh blackberry, dark cherry, cardamom, and sweet baking spices. On the palate, the wine exhibits flavors of sassafras and tobacco with a hint of earthiness. With its long, richly mineral finish and balanced, velvety tannins, the wine has garnered praise from both *Wine Spectator* and *Wine Enthusiast*. Saffron Fields Vineyard also supplies grapes to other Oregon wineries, creating multiple opportunities to experience this truly unique site.

The tasting room features sweeping views of the vineyards, thoughtfully designed Japanese gardens, and a sophisticated art collection. The tasting room and grounds integrate with the surrounding landscape to inspire an atmosphere of contemplation and ease. When working with their architect, Sanjeev and Angela insisted on using glass, wood, and water for their ability to evoke emotion through fluidity and serenity. Wanting to capture the history of the site, they ensured that all the wood from a barn that once stood on the site was salvaged and incorporated into the new facility. Their desire is to make the experience of visiting Saffron Fields a part of each guest's personal narrative—a part of their own Oregon wine country experience.

Top & Bottom: The contemporary architecture of the tasting room is warmed by the recovered wood ceiling and the art collection featuring artists such as Darren Almond, Jennifer Steinkamp, and Leo Villareal.

Middle: The video installation "Daisy Bell" by Jennifer Steinkamp cascades down the wall next to the bar. The windows look out over the vineyard and coastal range.

Facing Page: The Zen garden room features hand-blown fixtures by Esque Studios and views of the garden and vineyard.
Photographs by Andréa Johnson

Yamhill-Carlton Pinot Noir
Serve alongside lamb stew with root vegetables.

Tastings
Open to the public daily, year-round

SAFFRON FIELDS
Vineyard

Silvan Ridge Winery

Eugene

Overlooking a sea of vine-covered, tree-lined rolling hills, Silvan Ridge Winery is a lush respite for an afternoon of sipping award-winning wines and savoring the view. Located 15 miles southwest of downtown Eugene, the winery even takes its name from the backdrop of the surrounding area, as *silvan* is the Latin word for "wooded." Interestingly, Silva is also the maiden name of Carolyn Chambers, who really served as the founding matriarch of the winery.

Now helmed by her daughter, Elizabeth Chambers, the family-owned winery has a colorful history that dates back to 1979, when Hinman Vineyards first opened. It wasn't until 1991 though, that the Chambers clan put their unique mark on the business when Carolyn acquired Hinman, which was Oregon's top-selling winery at the time. That same year, the vineyard released the premium line of reserve wines under the Silvan Ridge label. Little did Liz know that when she was seated at the ensuing celebratory dinner—nine months pregnant with her daughter, no less—the birth of her future in the winemaking business was also taking shape.

Only two short years later, Liz took over the day-to-day management of Silvan Ridge, where she oversees the production of approximately 25,000 cases of premium varietals annually, including cabernet sauvignon, malbec, Muscat, pinot gris, pinot noir, syrah, and viognier. One of the top-selling wines, the Muscat Semi-Sparkling, was once served in the White House.

Top: Argentine winemaker JP Valot crafts the Silvan Ridge Malbec.

Bottom: Julia Stiltner is the daughter of Elizabeth Chambers.

Facing Page: Silvan Ridge Winery welcomes visitors daily.
Photographs by Andréa Johnson

"If you start with anything less than wonderful fruit, you will end up with less than wonderful wine," says Silvan Ridge's general manager and director of winemaking Jonathan Oberlander who, together with winemaker Juan Pablo Valot, takes a hands-on approach to ensure the quality of the product, from grape to glass. Adopting a style that combines classic European technique with the innovation of the new winemaking generation, the team crafts elegant wines that take advantage of the state's diverse climate and soil conditions.

While Silvan Ridge maintains a five-acre parcel of pinot gris, the winery also relies heavily on sourcing superior fruit from longtime growers all over the state of Oregon, with a focus on the favorable Willamette Valley in northern Oregon and the Rogue Valley in the south.

Silvan Ridge doesn't only produces premier wines, though. Liz supports the community through a number of local events, including Friday night concerts and the Silvan Ridge Twilight 5K Race. In addition, for more than 20 years, the winery has participated in the Winetasia fundraiser for the Children's Miracle Network.

What began as one of the early Oregon wineries has burgeoned into a destination that produces a compelling selection of the Northwest's most distinctive wines that are simultaneously expressive and subtle. Always striving to develop the complex balance between richness and delicacy, Silvan Ridge synergizes Old World traditions with New World techniques to achieve a masterfully blended final product.

Above Left: JP Valot is proud of his creations.
Photograph by Silvan Ridge Winery

Above Top: The beautiful banquet room overlooks lush vineyards.
Photograph by Silvan Ridge Winery

Above Bottom: Guests enjoy a glass of wine on the patio.
Photograph by Andréa Johnson

Facing Page: Owner Elizabeth Chambers shares her wines with guests in the tasting room.
Photograph by Andréa Johnson

WINE & FARE

Viognier
Perfect alongside Thai noodle salad.

Muscat Semi-Sparkling
Pairs vivaciously with pear citrus cobbler.

Malbec
Pairs beautifully with barbecue beef kabobs.

Tastings
Open to the public daily

Silvan Ridge
WINERY

2 0 1 1
OREGON
ROGUE VALLEY

MALBEC
Single Vineyard

Sokol Blosser Winery

Dayton

The year was 1970, and the wine industry in Oregon was practically non-existent. But that didn't stop Susan Sokol Blosser and Bill Blosser from pursuing their pinot dreams. The couple may not have been the most likely winemaking candidates, when the recent Stanford liberal arts graduates parked their '68 Volkswagen Camper at an abandoned prune orchard in the Dundee Hills of Dayton, Oregon, some 30 miles southwest of Portland. But little did they know they would become pioneers in the industry, planting crucial seeds for the future of Oregon wine.

With precious little farming experience and only basic winemaking knowledge, they instead let passion be their guide. Noticing some interesting climate similarities between the esteemed French wine region of Burgundy and the state of Oregon, their original goal was to successfully grow the temperamental pinot noir grape and thereby create world-class wine from their Dayton hub. They succeeded through a series of trial and error.

Now, Sokol Blosser Winery has grown to encompass 87 acres of organic vineyards. Careful hand-harvesting and sorting, fermentation in small lots, and aging 16 months in French oak all ensure that Sokol Blosser's specialty, pinot noir, receives the care and commitment it requires and deserves. The winery also produces other notable varietals, including Muscat, pinot gris, riesling, and the Evolution label of red, white, and sparkling wines.

Top: Co-presidents and siblings Alison Sokol Blosser and Alex Sokol Blosser relax among their wine barrels.
Photograph by Leah Nash

Bottom: Front porch of the Sokol Blosser Tasting Room with tableside service.
Photograph by Andréa Johnson

Facing Page: The Sokol Blosser Tasting Room was designed to be an extension of the region's terroir.
Photograph by Andréa Johnson

"Acid, complexity, and fruit come together in a very special way for pinot noir here in the Willamette Valley. When the growing season cooperates, this trifecta of flavor inspires the pinot noir drinkers of the world," says winemaker, and Susan and Bill's son, Alex Sokol Blosser.

In addition to exalting the glorious grape, Sokol Blosser has made a significant investment in sustainable architecture and environmentally friendly practices. One of the most significant points that informs the winery's philosophy is an innate respect for the land, with the belief that top-quality wine is a direct expression of the terroir. In another pioneering move, Sokol Blosser's barrel cellar was the first to be LEED certified in the United States in 2002, and the winery received full USDA organic certification three years later.

The winery was also the first in Oregon to open a purposefully built tasting room, which debuted in 1977. Named for the architect who designed the building, the John Storrs Tasting Room boasts sweeping views of the vineyards and still plays a charming role at the winery for small gatherings.

Top: The Sokol Blosser Tasting Room was designed by Allied Works Architecture.
Photograph by Andréa Johnson

Middle: Fall harvest season.
Photograph by Andréa Johnson

Bottom: Dundee Hills Pinot Noir.
Photograph by Michael Brown

Facing Page: Winemaker and co-president Alex Sokol Blosser tending to pinot noir grapes during harvest.
Photograph by Andréa Johnson

Sokol Blosser's second tasting room, which opened in 2013, also aligns with the good-to-the-earth values of the winery. The natural yet modern structure, designed by Allied Works, pays homage to the land and is indeed a reflection of it, with the all-wood structure acting as more of an extension of the rich surrounding scenery, rather than an incongruous addition to it. From traditional tastings in The Main Room, rich with light and views, to a more intimate experience in The Library, or perfectly paired courses in The Kitchen, the venue offers personalized opportunities to savor the wine, the warm hospitality, and the surrounding land.

With the second generation of Sokol Blossers now at the helm, the winery has become quite the family affair. Susan and Bill's three children, Nik, Alex, and Alison, grew up working in the family vineyards, so it's perhaps only natural that they returned to the business after brief stints away. In addition to serving as the winemaker, Alex, along with Alison, became co-presidents in 2008, with Nik as chairman of the board.

But the groundbreaking mission that began in the early '70s—with little more than a VW and a couple's dream—remains the same: To continue to push the envelope and produce world-class, sought-after wines, while respecting the land.

Above Left: The Library seats up to 12 for pinot noir education.

Above Top: The Kitchen space is perfect for food and wine pairings.

Above Bottom: A wine flight on the front porch.

Facing Page: The main room boasts stunning views of the Willamette Valley and Dundee Hills.
Photographs by Andréa Johnson

WINE & FARE

Willamette Valley Pinot Gris
Complex fruit, minerality, and vibrant acidity pair well with oysters and smoked fish.

Dundee Hills Pinot Noir
Red fruits, hints of spice, and earth match with roasted duck or wild mushroom tart.

Estate Cuvée Pinot Noir
The terroir-driven Burgundian-style pinot complements braised beef and roasted lamb.

White Riesling
Icewine-style with rich apricot and stunning acidity; pair with Rogue Creamery cheeses.

Tastings
Open to the public daily, year-round

Sokol Blosser Winery

Soter Vineyards

Carlton

Soter Vineyards makes its home in an unforgettable place called Mineral Springs Ranch, situated just east of Carlton in the northern Willamette Valley. Centuries-old oak trees grace the hillsides of the 240-acre property, which Tony and Michelle Soter had envisioned would become the site of one of Oregon's most spectacular vineyards more than a decade ago.

Tony began his winegrowing career in Napa Valley in the 1970s. While founding his own successful Etude Wines, he also made wine and consulted for iconic names like Araujo, Dalla Valle, Niebaum-Coppola, Shafer, Spottswoode, and Viader. During this time, Michelle pursued a career in advertising and marketing before coming to represent the wines of Moraga Vineyards in Los Angeles and then moving to Napa to focus on Etude Wines.

Native Oregonians, the couple found themselves called back to their home state for many reasons, not the least of which was a love for pinot noir. They sold Etude and turned their attention entirely to the Willamette Valley. Today the Mineral Springs vineyard consists of 30 acres of pinot noir and four acres of chardonnay and is thought by many to be one of the new benchmark sites for growing great pinot noir. The ranch is also home to hundreds of sheep, chickens, quail, and other animals, fruit orchards, a vegetable farm, grassland, forest, and great people—all of which come together to make Mineral Springs a hive of creative activity.

The biodiversity of the ranch provides the vineyard with a more natural spectrum of organisms, which is a fundamental advantage when focusing on organic and biodynamic farming. The dedication to sustainability at Soter Vineyards starts in the vineyard but is also evident in the packaging, commitment to solar energy, building designs, and through the goal of sustaining a happy and healthy staff.

Top: Wine pioneers Michelle and Tony Soter are passionate stewards of the land as well as lovers of great wine, notably pinot noir, chardonnay, and sparkling wine.

Bottom: Soter's estate-grown Mineral Springs Ranch and Mineral Springs Pinot Noirs come from the 30 acres of sustainably farmed vineyard in the Yamhill-Carlton AVA.

Facing Page: Cradled by 34 acres of pinot noir and chardonnay, the lodge at Mineral Springs Ranch is host to daily tastings and special events.
Photographs by Andréa Johnson

Soter Vineyards produces three labels of wine: the Estate wines, sourced exclusively from the Mineral Springs vineyard; North Valley Vineyards wines, and Planet Oregon Pinot Noir. Started in 2007, North Valley Vineyards is a partnership between Tony and Michelle Soter, winemaker James Cahill, and sales and marketing director Brian Sypher. A prominent marque in the ever-growing landscape of Oregon wine, North Valley focuses on the production of exceptional pinot noir and chardonnay through the purchasing of fruit from noteworthy vineyards in the northern Willamette Valley. All of its farmer-grower partnerships share a dedication to great wine and a healthier future through certified sustainable agriculture. Meanwhile, Planet Oregon takes the same message statewide with wines that are delicious, affordable, and responsibly grown.

At Soter Vineyards, the mission is to make world class wines with every vintage. The wines represent the character of each site, region, and season as a precious expression of a distinct place and time. They pursue the tradition of growing and crafting compelling wines with the unmistakable identity of Oregon's Willamette Valley and, most specifically, the Mineral Springs vineyard.

Above: The Mineral Springs vineyard benefits from ideal temperatures and extended sunlight hours making the resulting wines well balanced and beautiful, much like the place in which they are grown.

Left: North Valley partners James Cahill and Brian Sypher join the Soters to create regionally-focused wines that celebrate the diversity of the northern Willamette Valley.

Facing Page: Guests enjoy an afternoon of tasting and expansive views at the lodge at Soter Vineyards, Mineral Springs Ranch.
Photographs by Andréa Johnson

WINE & FARE

Mineral Springs Ranch Pinot Noir
Pair with pit-roasted lamb and spring vegetables.

North Valley Reserve Chardonnay
Best served with grilled quail with chanterelles.

Mineral Springs Ranch Brut Rose
Serve with fresh Northwestern oysters with rhubarb mignonette.

North Valley Pinot Noir
Delicious with cedar-plank wild salmon with honey and rosemary.

Tastings
By appointment only

SOTER
MINERAL SPRINGS
—————⋄—————
Pinot Noir

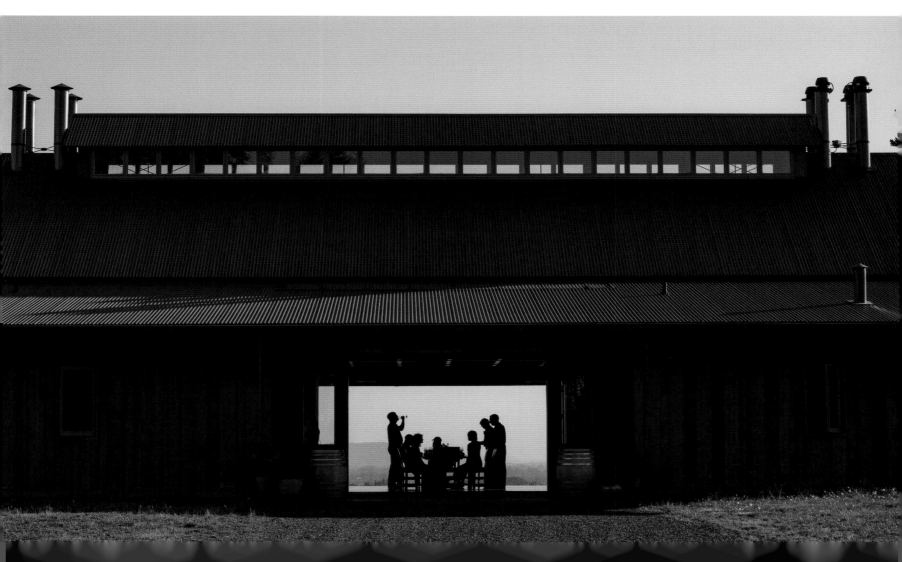

Spindrift Cellars

Philomath

Often described as "strikingly original" or "the little winery that could," Spindrift Cellars certainly lives up to its tributes. Owned and run by winemaker Matthew Compton and his wife, Tabitha, the urban winery in downtown Philomath maintains a reputation for wines that are fruit forward, earthy, and expressive of the local vineyards that produce them.

After moving to Oregon at the age of 22, Matthew went to work for Oregon State University managing a research farm for wine grapes. The New Jersey native and father of three then launched his vineyard management company, Small World Wine Company. He created his first vintage in 2003 and moved into Spindrift's current facility a year later. Since then, Spindrift wines have garnered many awards and recognitions, including ratings of 90 and above, while being been selected as Best Buy and Top 100 Best Buys of the World by *Wine & Spirits, Wine Spectator*, and *Wine Enthusiast* magazines.

Matt and Tabitha have built their winery business with both passion and intelligence. They focus on producing crisp, quality wines that display the true varietal characteristics of the grape, bolstered by a sustainable farming foundation. As Spindrift has grown, the couple's labor of love continues to produce a full line of nationally recognized fine wines, offered at consumer-friendly prices. "We're showing more of what the vineyards can do in our area, in the heart of the Willamette Valley," says Matthew. "They're true to variety, they're bright and fragrant, and well-received by consumers. People enjoy them."

Top: Winemaker Matthew Compton walks DeerHaven Vineyard in Philomath. Matt has been managing vineyards and farming sustainably in the Willamette Valley since 1995.

Bottom: The next generation of vintners: Kael, Porter, and Odin Compton.

Facing Page: Tasting room manager Tabitha Compton pours a fine Oregon pinot noir in the Spindrift Cellars tasting room. *Photographs by Andréa Johnson*

Stangeland Vineyards and Winery

Salem

When Larry Miller began working in the industrial sector after college, he had no idea that a nine-month trip to Europe a few years later would lead to a series of opportunities that eventually culminated in the planting of a vineyard and the starting of a winery outside Salem, Oregon. The trip inspired a love of wine and cuisine, so that when the chance to purchase a little rural country store near his hometown of Salem presented itself, Larry jumped at the chance. Through a mutual friend, Larry met Dave Lett of Oregon's iconic Eyrie Vineyards in 1974. Dave asked Larry if he wanted to come along on a consultation of some nearby land that showed a potential for producing wine grapes. This introduction to the industry stuck with Larry, and soon after that, he began selling Lett's wine in his small store.

Larry's love of wine didn't stop at selling it though, and the idea to purchase vineyard land was continually at the forefront of his mind. One day, Larry bounced some ideas off of his mother and she informed him that she and his father owned about five acres with a sloped, southern exposure in West Salem. The difficult-to-access plot of land—there wasn't even a road that led into it—was virtually untouched and appeared to be absolutely perfect. About a year later, Larry, along with his brother and sister, began laying the foundation for Stangeland Vineyards and Winery. In the spring of 1976, the trio planted cuttings purchased from Dave Lett in Larry's sister's garden while still working their day jobs. As with many endeavors, life goes on, and Larry was unable to move the grapevines until they were fully mature two years later. But move them they did, and soon about half of the family's land was planted with wine grapes: the Wädenswil clone of pinot noir and chardonnay.

Top: Lily of the Nile is in bloom at the winery.
Photograph by Andréa Johnson

Bottom: The basalt columns are fondly referred to as "Stangehenge."
Photograph by Ron Cooper

Facing Page: The winery proudly flies the American and Norwegian flags.
Photograph by Ron Cooper

The early years were humble; the small, family-managed crew ran a 600-foot hose from the neighboring property to the vines to hand-water the grapes a couple of times each year. Even with the relocation and the tenuous beginnings for the grapes, about 95 percent of the original planting of pinot noir survived. As the fifth oldest planting in the AVA, Stangeland was one of the very few planted vineyards that only covered about 25 acres of the Eola-Amity Hills. In 1982, four short rows of pinot gris were added; the 45 plants were given to Larry by a neighboring grower with a surplus. In 1983, a small two-story house was built which enabled Larry to manage the small vineyard. By 1986, the pinot gris was thriving and Larry decided to fill out the remaining acre-and-a-quarter with this up-and-coming varietal. Eight hundred plants were purchased from Lett's vineyard manager, Joel Myers. Then, in 1988, along with four other friends, Larry purchased a de-stemmer and a small basket press. For three years, amateur wine was made by this group who called themselves the "Wine Guild." The Guild produced barrel-sized batches of wines that performed well at the Oregon State Fair, earning the group a few local awards.

Pronounced as "stang-land," Stangeland Vineyards was named for Larry's maternal grandparents who emigrated from Norway. Literally translated, Stangeland means "strong land" which seemed appropriate for the rocky basalt base of the vineyard site. For a time, Stangeland was still primarily a grape grower, with the majority of the vineyards' grapes sold to several local wineries to augment its own wines. In order to fulfill his dream of owning a full-production winery, Larry shut his contracting business down and went back to work for the company he'd worked for right out of college. When his workday finished at four o'clock, he would be out among the grapes. The time investment paid off. In the same year Stangeland was established—1991—the first vintages of chardonnay, pinot gris, and pinot noir were made: a whopping 140 cases total.

Left: The winery building's large doors are made of 100-year-old Douglas fir recycled lumber.
Photograph by Ron Cooper

During every year of its production, Stangeland has crafted very small lots of exquisite wine to include estate and single vineyard pinot noirs that showcase the terroir of the Eola-Amity Hills AVA. In 2000, Stangeland received a solicitation from the European wine competition, Mondial du Pinot Noir, held in Sierre, Switzerland. The 1998 Pinot Noir Winemaker's Estate Reserve was honored with a gold medal that year, and the winery has gone on to win two more gold medals and three silver medals, the only Oregon winery to ever do so, ranking it among some of the best wineries in the world.

Larry enjoys sharing his experience and knowledge with the next generation of winemakers. He and his wife Ruth play host to grape growers and training winemakers whenever the opportunity presents itself. Such burgeoning experts hail from across the globe, and these international relationships are a source of pride and joy for the Millers. Sustainability is also important at Stangeland, where a line of grapevines is used naturally to combat soil erosion along the property's edge. Larry's practical approach to winemaking means that the vineyards are farmed to LIVE standards. Guests are invited to visit the winery's tasting room weekends, year-round, and daily June through November.

Above: Ruth and Larry relax on the deck with their lakeland terrier, Bobi.
Photograph by Andréa Johnson

Top Left: The owners enjoy a quiet moment in Ruth's rose garden.
Photograph by Andréa Johnson

Bottom Left: The Vintners House at Stangeland Vineyards is a beautiful B&B.
Photograph by Larry Miller

Facing Page: Sunrise is spectacular after an early autumn snowfall.
Photograph by Larry Miller

WINE & FARE

Estate Reserve Pinot Noir
Serve alongside chicken with morels and tarragon cream sauce, grilled salmon, or pork roast with nut stuffing.

Eola-Amity Hills Pinot Gris
Perfect alongside spicy Asian dishes, seared seafood, or shrimp salad.

Stangeland Chardonnay
Pairs well with fresh sea scallops in a butter sauce, asparagus, and wild mushroom risotto.

Tastings
Open to the public, Friday through Sunday

Stangeland **Vineyards**

2012
Pinot Noir
Eola-Amity Hills
Willamette Valley
Estate Reserve

Red Wine/Vin Rouge

Sweet Earth Vineyards

Monroe

Premium, limited-edition, estate-grown wines are the focus of Sweet Earth Vineyards, established in 2005. The wines and the winery itself have earned both industry accolades and a loyal following of "Sweet Earthlings" who make the winery a frequent stop on their travels. It's a family affair at Sweet Earth, and that's part of its charm. Former educators Phil and Nancy McCullum combined their love of fine wine and the desire for a rural lifestyle to create an inviting tasting room where visitors are welcomed like members of the family. Along with their children, Justin, Kamala, and Michele and her husband, Mike, the McCullums have nurtured the vines and created a unique tasting experience that guests don't soon forget.

Ideally nestled on a south-facing slope under the protection of Mary's Peak and Oregon's Coast Range, Sweet Earth Vineyards' well-drained Jory soils are perfect for pinot noir and pinot gris grapes. Under the direction of veteran winemaker Matt Compton, these grapes are transformed into small-lot premium wines. Every decision—from the music played in the tasting room to the precise production of each vintage—is a hands-on experience, making Sweet Earth Vineyards a distinctive artisan producer of award-winning Oregon pinot noir and pinot gris. Each year, the winery hosts Quilts in the Vineyard, an outdoor quilt show on Labor Day weekend. More than 100 quilts are featured, along with a wine-themed quilt created by Nancy and her Old School Quilters group that is raffled to benefit Strengthening Rural Families in Benton County.

Top: Double Gold and Best of Show are among the many awards recognizing the fine artisan wines produced with exceptional fruit grown in Sweet Earth's estate vineyards.

Middle: Work becomes play when friends and family get together for the annual harvest at Sweet Earth Vineyards.

Bottom: Wine club members, known affectionately as "Sweet Earthlings," relax with a glass of fine wine in the party and picnic pavilion where musicians are often hosted.

Facing Page: From the old-growth forest to the vineyard landscape, nature's beauty abounds, creating another glorious day at the vineyard. Come swirl, sip, and savor the flavor.
Photographs by Robert Holmes

WillaKenzie Estate

Yamhill

For Bernard Lacroute, there are a few principles that are fundamental and absolutely necessary to create a great wine: the place and its soil, and the knowledge and passion of the people who create it. The way a wine looks, smells, and dances on the tongue reflects the place from which the grapes are grown. Embracing simple, pure, Old World philosophies and New World innovation, the team at WillaKenzie Estate creates wines that speak of the unique terroir of the estate, and the pioneering spirit of Oregon wine country and their French roots.

A native of the southern Burgundy region in France, Bernard was raised with wine as an integral part of everyday life. He has always been an avid gardener, so after many years in the high-tech world, owning a winery not only sounded like the perfect second career, but a dream come true. Partial to pinot noir because it is what he grew up with, Bernard's only real question was where to purchase land for a vineyard and winery. After trips to New Zealand and California, he was struck by the climate and soil of Oregon—it is stunningly similar to the cool-climate regions of Burgundy. He also found a sense of adventure in Oregon where the grapes are absolutely dependent on the climate. According to Bernard, the experience can be nail-biting at times, but with the right amount of patience, great wines result.

Top: Proprietor Bernard Lacroute stands on top of "Big Foot," the unique punch-down technology he designed.

Bottom: Estate winemaker Thibaud Mandet is ready to punch down the grapes with "Big Foot."

Facing Page: WillaKenzie Estate has views of Mount St. Helens.
Photographs by Andréa Johnson

It is clear that Bernard, winemaker Thibaud Mandet, and the rest of the team at WillaKenzie possess this virtue. The wines express the flavors and aromas gained from their natural environment. Purity and expression of the varietal, and the specificity created by the site, is what it is all about. In fact, Thibaud and Bernard know exactly which part of the vineyard each barrel of wine originated from. Guided by this Old World concept—Thibaud is himself from Auvergne, France—the winemaking team at WillaKenzie adds American ingenuity to the practice whenever possible. The winery operates an automated punch-down device designed by Bernard and a state-of-the-art chilling facility, while embracing sustainable techniques that care for the soil as illustrated by certifications such as those through Oregon Certified Sustainable Wines, LIVE, and Salmon-Safe. The winery remains true to Old World techniques with its gravity-flow winery and French oak barrels. Even the name of the estate reflects the terroir. It is named after the sedimentary soil, which derived its name from the nearby Willamette and McKenzie rivers.

Above: WillaKenzie Estate's vineyards, forest, and pasture are picturesque.

Right: Bernard demonstrates how "Big Foot" punches down the grapes.

Facing Page: The puncheon is being filled with grapes, de-stemmed by hand, for the Grand Reserve Pinot Noir bottling.
Photographs by Andréa Johnson

Reflecting the philosophy of combining the traditional with the modern, WillaKenzie was one of the first wineries in Oregon to plant both traditional and new Dijon clones of pinot noir. With more than 12 different clones of pinot noir planted at the WillaKenzie vineyard, the portfolio of wine displays a wide range of diversity. In addition to pinot noir, WillaKenzie Estate makes chardonnay, gamay noir, pinot blanc, pinot gris, and pinot meunier.

The Aliette Pinot Noir is one of the estate-grown wines crafted by WillaKenzie Estate. Ruby red in color, its luxurious bouquet of dried violets, strawberry, lavender, and hints of cedar makes it a wine that is delectable from the first whiff. The wine displays a fine balance between its graceful yet powerful palate. The 2009 bottling earned a gold medal and was named best in show by *Decanter* magazine, where it was judged as the top pinot noir in the nation over 10,000 other wines in the Decanter World Wine Awards.

Visitors to WillaKenzie Estate are invited to sample the award-winning wines during relaxed tastings at the beautiful tasting room on the estate. Guests can also walk through the vineyards and the winery, taking in the panoramic views while learning about the entire winemaking process. Private tours and tastings include wine and cheese pairings, an exploration of the winery's sensory garden, and a sampling of the coveted Reserve Pinot Noir.

Top: WillaKenzie Cellar Club members enjoying wine and the view on the tasting room patio.

Bottom: The Texas longhorns enjoy the pasture as part of the winery's certified sustainable ecosystem.

Facing Page: Standing proudly beside the vineyard-designated pinot noirs and holding a bit of WillaKenzie soil, Bernard shows that dirt really matters.
Photographs by Andréa Johnson

WINE & FARE

WillaKenzie Estate Emery Pinot Noir
Pairs beautifully with barbecued lamb chops.

WillaKenzie Estate Pierre Leon
Serve alongside grilled salmon, scallops, or goat cheese
and chicken pizza.

WillaKenzie Estate Pinot Gris
Pairs elegantly with Thai smoked salmon and grilled asparagus.

WillaKenzie Estate Terres Basses Pinot Noir
Pairs well with duck breast with hoisin prune sauce
or marinated pepper steak.

Tastings
Open to the public daily

Willamette Valley Vineyards

Turner

When Richard Sommer graduated from UC Davis and decided to establish the first post-Prohibition winery in Oregon, he consulted a lawyer to ensure he had all the correct state and federal licenses before proceeding. That lawyer's son turned out to be Jim Bernau, founder of Willamette Valley Vineyards. Helping to fulfill his father's prophetic prediction that someday grapevines would cover Oregon, Jim purchased the original estate in 1983. The old pioneer plum orchard was covered by blackberry vines, but Jim soon planted chardonnay, pinot gris, and pinot noir, watering the vines by hand with 17 lengths of 75-foot garden hose up and down the vineyard rows. Today the winery spans across three vineyards and produces some of the finest estate pinot noir in the region.

Both his education at UC Davis and his attendance at seminars in Burgundy, France, prepared Jim for the first production of wine from his vineyards in 1989. Through careful canopy management, tending to everything from the choice of rootstock to the sustainable practices, Willamette produces distinctive wines that reflect the terroir of the Willamette Valley. On the gentle hill of the original estate vineyard just south of Salem, Oregon, luscious grapes grow in the iron-rich, volcanic Jory and Nekia soils on a 12-degree slope facing the sun. Its clay loam provides a soft bed for the roots, retaining moisture for the entirety of its two to five feet of depth. The 69 acres are home to Dijon clones grafted in 1993 to produce both pinot noir and chardonnay clusters.

Top: Jim Bernau, founder of Willamette Valley Vineyards, which offers a unique wine tasting experience for guests from all over the world. Since 1983, Jim has resided on the property, perfecting the vineyards and winemaking techniques.
Photograph by Carolyn Wells-Kramer

Bottom: The Estate Pinot Noir is the winery's signature wine. It truly expresses the terroir of the three unique vineyard sites within the Willamette Valley that contribute to this bottling: Tualatin Estate Vineyard, Elton Vineyard, and the Estate Vineyard.
Photograph by Andréa Johnson

Facing Page: Nestled into the slopes of the Eola-Amity Hills AVA, Elton Vineyard provides beautiful fruit for the pinot noir. First planted in 1983, the 60-acre vineyard is surrounded by Jory and Nekia soils and was named one of Oregon's top 10 vineyards by *Wine Press Northwest*.
Photograph by Andréa Johnson

Like Willamette's Estate Vineyard, the Tualatin Estate Vineyard is located in the Willamette Valley appellation. Established in 1973 by one of Oregon's first emigrating Napa Valley winemakers, Bill Fuller, Tualatin is one of the oldest vineyards in the valley. Named after the local Tualatin River, scores of grapevines appear to gently flow down the hilly slopes—Tualatin means "gentle and easy flowing" and is a word from the indigenous people of the region. One hundred acres of pinot noir take up the majority of the vineyard space at Tualatin, the rest being planted with four acres of chardonnay, 23 acres of riesling, five acres of gewürztraminer, 10 acres of Muscat, nine acres of pinot blanc, and 15 acres of pinot gris, among others. Newer plantings include seven different French clones that are twice as dense as the original vineyards. Most of the soil that covers the vineyard is Laurelwood. This soil is unique to Oregon and is formed over thousands of years on layers of wind-blown, glacial silt called loess. Deposits of iron concentrations called pisolites riddle the top layer and are caused by the weathering of minerals in the soil. Well drained and gently sloping, Tualatin continues to produce award-winning wines.

Elton Vineyards in the Eola-Amity Hills sub-appellation is owned by Dick and Betty O'Brien, who originally planted grapes on the land inherited from Betty's parents, Elton and Peggy Ingram. In 2007, the O'Briens wished to retire and a long-term lease to Willamette Valley Vineyards was contracted. The majority of these east-southeast slopes is planted in pinot noir, accompanied by Dijon-clone chardonnay, pinot gris, and a small amount of grüner veltliner grapes. Like all the vineyards under the ownership and management of Willamette Valley Vineyards, Elton is certified sustainable and recognized by both Salmon-Safe and LIVE.

In 2008, LIVE presented Jim with the organization's first Founders' Award for "his service to sustainability in the Oregon wine industry."

Top: The grapes at the winery's three vineyard locations are an exclusive product of the different native soils found in Oregon. The unique process used to harvest these grapes drives much of the success of the winery.

Bottom: The annual Oregon Grape Stomp Championship event is an opportunity for wine enthusiasts around the country to participate in the harvest celebration. Guests often arrive in costume to have fun and compete in one of the most anticipated events at Willamette Valley Vineyards.

Facing Page: Tualatin Estate Vineyard is one of the oldest and most respected vineyard sites in Oregon's Willamette Valley. One hundred seventy four acres of vineyards stretch over this site in Forest Grove, Oregon, and have produced world-renowned wines for more than 40 years.
Photographs by Andréa Johnson

As the leading producer of Oregon Certified Sustainable Wine, Jim was honored as the recipient of the 2012 Award of Merit by the American Wine Society. Under his careful watch, Willamette is the first winery in the world to use sustainable corks that are certified to Forest Stewardship Council standards by the Rainforest Alliance. The winery is also the first to receive Salmon-Safe's Hero of Salmon design award. In addition, Jim has gifted Oregon State University with funds to create the first endowed professorship in fermentation science in the US.

Above: The Barrel Room Terrace, used by the winemaking staff for blending, also offers an indoor and outdoor area where guests can enjoy the breathtaking views with a glass of wine or host private events and dinners.
Photograph by Andréa Johnson

Right: Described as a farmer's best friend, owls are a natural way to control the moles and voles that dig around the base of grapevines. With the aid of the Cascades Raptor Center, Willamette Valley Vineyards has now introduced more than 20 rehabilitated owls and kestrels into its three estate vineyards.
Photograph by Matt Boyington

Facing Page Bottom: Head winemaker Don Crank III assistant winemaker Daniel Shepherd, and their production crew are supported in the cellar by winemakers Drew Voit and Isabelle Meunier, and also Tualatin Estate founder and winemaker Bill Fuller.
Photograph by Andréa Johnson

Previous Pages: Laurelwood is the soil that covers most of Tualatin Estate. The depth and good drainage of Laurelwood allow deep rooting of the grapevines, and the clays accumulated in the subsoils can provide reserves of late season water.
Photograph by Andréa Johnson

Recognized as one of the Top 100 Wineries in 2011 by *Wine & Spirits Magazine*, Willamette was also named Oregon Winery of the Year in the same year by *Wine Press Northwest*. The winery holds the distinction of being a television celebrity, featured on an episode of Rachael Ray's "$40 a Day," which airs on Food Network. A favorite of NBC chef Inger Johnson, bottles of Willamette pinot noir repeatedly appeared on the set of "Friends," and more recently on the set of NBC's "Grimm."

Willamette's flagship wine, the Estate Pinot Noir, is a classic representation of the Willamette Valley AVA terroir, presenting the nose with aromas of cherry, pie spice, baked apples, and brown sugar, accented with a hint of cinnamon. Brandied cherry and dark-chocolate flavors mingle on the palate with a spicy finish. Rated as a 93, the wine is described as earthy and dark with a savory herbal quality by *Wine & Spirits Magazine*.

With a dedication to sustainable viticulture and winemaking, Jim, winemaker Don Crank, and assistant winemaker Daniel Shepherd create food-friendly, distinctive wines that satisfy even the most discerning palates.

Guests are invited to taste these beautiful wines at the winery daily in the grand Estate Tasting Room. There a personal winery ambassador assists visitors on a tour and educational wine and food pairing selection. From that point forward, guests have a personal point of contact at the winery who is never more than a phone call away, ready to choose the perfect bottle even from remote locations around the globe.

Above Left: The pairings menu, developed by winery chef Eric Nelson, offers seasonal and local dishes for guests to enjoy with their favorite wines.
Photograph by Matt Boyington

Above Top: As if the views from the winery were not spectacular enough, add another six stories. The tower is visible from just about anywhere on the property and offers a beautiful panoramic view of the Willamette Valley.
Photograph by Andréa Johnson

Above Bottom: The view from inside the winery's signature tower, which Jim modeled after historic Oregon fire lookouts with the intention to provide guests a visually stunning explanation of why the Willamette Valley is an extraordinary region to grow pinot noir.
Photograph by Andréa Johnson

Facing Page: The tasting room offers a warm and inviting environment, complete with a cozy fireplace and a chef's demonstration counter with a wood and vine-burning oven.
Photograph by Andréa Johnson

Bernau Block Pinot Noir
Serve with rack of Oregon lamb or smoked duck and mushroom risotto.

Estate Pinot Noir
Pairs beautifully with complexly spiced dishes such as cracked black pepper salmon or roasted five-spice pork tenderloin.

Estate Chardonnay
Perfect alongside chicken dishes with white sauces, pork roast, and creamy pasta dishes.

Pinot Gris
Pairs elegantly with seafood dishes such as Pacific Dungeness crab, grilled halibut, salmon, and oysters.

Tastings
Open to the public daily, year-round

WILLAMETTE VALLEY
VINEYARDS

Winderlea Vineyard and Winery

Dundee

Like the anticipatory next chapter of a page-turning book, the story of Winderlea Vineyard and Winery is woven with a bit of adventure, romance, and a dash of the unexpected. The main characters are Winderlea's founders, Donna Morris and Bill Sweat—and pinot noir, of course. A shared love of food and wine has always been a meaningful part of Donna and Bill's relationship, from their first dates in the early 1980s at old school wine shops in the North End and Beacon Hill neighborhoods of Boston, Massachusetts. Subsequent epicurean escapes to noted wine regions and an exploration of myriad pinot noirs from across the country led to the collective realization that their favorite American pinot noirs were from Oregon.

Eventually, the siren call of the perfect sip was too strong to ignore for the couple. In 2006, they exchanged their Bostonian backgrounds for a more bucolic setting in Dundee, Oregon. That same year, they produced their first vintage. It was a quick turn, but Bill had planted roots in the winemaking business two years earlier, when he started researching the industry, taking viticulture and enology courses and participating in a Napa Valley harvest.

Although Winderlea is a boutique winery with a precious 16.5 acres, it yields a distinct and varied palate of fruit. The vineyards were originally planted in the 1970s, with a section replanted beginning in the late '90s, allowing for a mix of newer and more mature grapes using six different selections of pinot noir on three varying rootstock. The variety is a virtual playground for winemaker, Robert Brittan, who has much to work with when crafting the most noteworthy blends.

Top: Bill and Celie are out for a daily inspection of the vineyard just after harvest.

Bottom: Winderlea's highly regarded Legacy Pinot Noir is sourced from the oldest and most distinctive vines on the estate, dating back to 1974.

Facing Page: The modern and sustainable tasting room is surrounded by estate vineyards and features magnificent views of Mount Hood.
Photographs by Andréa Johnson

Specializing in small, premier lots of pinot noir and chardonnay, Winderlea reflects the highest quality, artisan winemaking with vintages that not only showcase the best characteristics of the vineyard, but also responsible stewardship of the land demonstrated by the property's LIVE certification and biodynamic farming practices.

As lovers of food, Donna and Bill ensure that their product pairs beautifully with fare, always serving as its complement, not as a source of competition. The nuanced complexity of the wine has both elegant and feminine notes with subtle layers of fruit, earthiness, and spice balanced with acidity. Even the name of the winery echoes a romantic quality. It shares its appellation with an idyllic Vermont property owned by the couple.

Visitors to Winderlea can enjoy a wine flight, or perhaps a meal, at the property's tasting room, which is nearly as seductive as the wine. Situated at the top of the property, the thoughtfully constructed space offers 360-degree views of the vineyards. The contemporary, glass-centric design also creates the illusion of an indoor-outdoor space that seemingly floats over the vines.

The tasting room is equipped with a commercial kitchen, which has attracted esteemed chefs for Winderlea's annual Summer Lunchtime Series and signature winemaker dinners. Donna and Bill have been committed to the winemaking community through their longtime support of Salud!. They donate a significant portion of their tasting room fees and participate in this Oregon wine auction that provides health care funding to the region's seasonal vineyard workers and their families.

Top: Bill and Donna share their lives, the vineyard, and hospitality duties with labradoodles Monty and Celie.

Middle: An intimate harvest winemaker's dinner at Winderlea features views of the estate and neighboring vineyards.

Bottom: Wine tasting is especially delightful on the deck.

Facing Page: Winderlea's estate vineyard and tasting room are picturesque.
Photographs by Andréa Johnson

Chardonnay
Perfect alongside peach caprese salad
with fresh mozzarella, basil, and mint.

Legacy Pinot Noir
Pairs beautifully with cherry wood smoked leg of lamb,
served with sweet potato-chèvre Napoleon and Brussels sprout leaves.

Vineyard Pinot Noir
The sublime companion to slow-roasted wild salmon
on braised endive with bacon lardons.

Tastings
Open to the public daily

Winter's Hill Estate

Dayton

When Peter and Emily Gladhart took stock of their 150-acre farm in the Dundee Hills, they realized the terrain was prime real estate for grape growing. And so they did just that, planting 21 acres of vineyards in 1990 and launching the now well-established and family-operated winery, Winter's Hill Estate.

The Gladharts allowed their grapes to flourish for a full decade, cultivating character-driven mature fruit. Their patience resulted in 298 cases of pinot noir in 1998, the estate's first vintage. It showcased the Dundee Hills terroir, one of Oregon wine country's most densely planted areas. One of the first vineyards to be established there, Winter's Hill features the defining characteristics of the Dundee Hills—Jory soils and gentle south-facing slopes. It looks out over the Willamette Valley and toward the Coast Range, benefiting from full sunshine during summer months and cool evening breezes that aid in the fruit's ripening and flavor development. The surrounding acreage is abundant with wildlife that resides in the Oregon White Oak and Douglas fir trees, with heritage oak savanna and native Willamette Valley prairie in restorative stages—a state recognized effort at Winter's Hill.

Top: On a September morning, Winter's Hill Estate is like an island in a sea of fog, looking south over the Willamette Valley.
Photograph by Shawn Linnehan

Bottom: Peter Gladhart and his wife, Emily, planted the first vineyards at Winter's Hill in 1990. Peter is responsible for managing all of the estate vineyards.
Photograph by Shawn Linnehan

Facing Page: The winery's relationship with Equestrian Wine Tours has allowed guests from around the world to experience the vineyard on horseback. Sarah Hahn leads the Gladharts on an October ride.
Photograph by Andréa Johnson

In 2004, Peter and Emily's son, Russell, joined the business along with his wife, Delphine. Russell had been a part of the winery since its inception when he was 18 years old and had also worked at vineyards and wineries around Oregon and as far-reaching as New Zealand. Meanwhile, Delphine honed her skills in France's Beaujolais and Burgundy regions, later pursuing an apprenticeship across the seas, in Oregon no less, where the couple met. Delphine joined the ranks as head winemaker, exhibiting a talent for developing the perfect palate and chemistry within the wine as well as overseeing blending and barrel selection. Her background has heavily influenced the Gladharts' thoughts on wine's acid structure, creating bottles of pinot noir that are known for their ability to develop and improve over the years.

The two generations blend harmoniously. Peter runs the vineyard while Emily works primarily in sales and marketing. Delphine crafts the wine, and Russell oversees the winery's operations. Winery events are family-centric productions and guests enjoy a horseback vineyard tour with Equestrian Wine Tours, or a barrel tasting with Delphine or Russell.

Left: Built into the hillside, the winery enjoys sweeping views of the Willamette Valley and the Coast Range. A dusting of snow celebrates sunset on New Year's Day.
Photograph by Craig Markham

In 2009, Winter's Hill evolved into a fully functional winery with the addition of an on-site facility. Built into the hillside, the building is as efficient as it is effective. The super-insulated walls are 15 inches thick for energy conservation when it comes to heating and cooling. Gravity plays an important role in the winemaking process as the fermentation tanks lie right below the crush area and grapes are able to fall naturally downward eliminating further handling. And the entire building was designed to be forklift-friendly in an ability to streamline the process.

The wines of Winter's Hill, which include pinot blanc, pinot gris, pinot noir, and rosé of pinot noir, are crafted with the highest degree of care and attention. The team is very gentle in their fermentation techniques, and each block of fruit is kept separate in order to highlight the exclusive flavors from that particular portion of the vineyard. Temperatures are mild and moderate, as artificial chilling or heating is kept to a minimum. Pinot noir is fermented in small open tanks then aged in oak barrels for at least 18 months, allowing the full character and complexity of the wine to develop. White wines are gently pressed without de-stemming, then fermented in stainless steel tanks and kept fresh so the fruit characters are highlighted.

Winter's Hill produces around 3,000 cases each year, with room to spare. There's additional space available in the winery and more land to plant vineyards. Russell says chardonnay is a possibility, but it's all about the timing. "It's not a business for someone who's impatient," he says. "To see it continue to grow through the generations keeps me pretty inspired."

Top: Winter's Hill is best known for its rich, complex pinot noir. All of the wines are made with fruit grown in the estate vineyards.
Photograph by Shawn Linnehan

Middle: Russell, Emily, and Peter enjoy a break during harvest. The grapes are hand-picked and quickly transported to the winery in small bins.
Photograph by Shawn Linnehan

Bottom: Winemaker Delphine Gladhart loads pinot gris into the press. Raised in Lyon, France, Delphine learned winemaking in Burgundy.
Photograph by Shawn Linnehan

Facing Page: Delphine, Russell, Emily, and Peter own and operate Winter's Hill.
Photograph by Andréa Johnson

Pinot Blanc Dundee Hills Estate
Pairs well with crab cakes.

Pinot Gris Dundee Hills Estate
Pairs well with poached salmon.

Pinot Noir Dundee Hills Estate
Pairs well with braised beef with roasted carrots and parsnips.

Rosé of Pinot Noir
Pairs well with grilled chicken breast over a green salad.

Tastings
Open to the public Wednesday through Monday

WINTER'S HILL
vineyard

2 0 · 1 2

PINOT NOIR
Block 5
DUNDEE HILLS, OREGON

ESTATE BOTTLED

ALC. 14.5% BY VOL.

Yamhill Valley Vineyards

McMinnville

It was 1982 when Denis Burger and his wife, Elaine McCall, first laid eyes on a beautiful 34-acre parcel nestled in the Coast Range foothills of Yamhill County. Located in the McMinnville area, it touted some of the oldest and most complex terroir in the acclaimed Willamette Valley. And they absolutely fell in love. After purchasing the land, the couple—along with close friend David Hinrichs—proceeded to cultivate their hillsides by planting the vineyards, expanding the property and developing their aptly named winery, Yamhill Valley Vineyards.

Yamhill is one of the oldest vineyard and winery estates in the Willamette Valley. The property now encompasses 150 acres, 105 of which are primarily planted with the pinot noir family of grapes. The pinot noir from the 1983 vintage placed first in the famous 1985 Oregon-Burgundy Challenge, and since then the wines have continued to garner awards at prestigious competitions nationwide. The wine's bold yet elegant style is distinguished by rich, black fruit characteristics. These are largely due to the marine sedimentary soils that dominate the site, while the minority volcanic soils add hi-toned, red fruit highlights. The resulting wines have dark color, tight structure, and lush, forward fruit.

Top: Tall Poppy is the top-of-the-line pinot noir bottling, only made in the very finest vintages.

Bottom: Pinot blanc grapes are nearing harvest.

Facing Page: The winery is surrounded by vineyards.
Photographs by Andréa Johnson

From evaluating the soil characteristics to studying the weather patterns and experimenting with crushing techniques, Denis never hesitates to make adjustments to their methods. A strong background in science doesn't hurt, either. Prior to owning a vineyard, both Denis and Elaine earned PhDs, working in scientific research and academia for two decades. Denis then managed four different biotech companies and continues to serve on the board of several. However, as much science as there is involved, he admits that producing a good bottle of wine is a very fine art. "You have to have a vision of the product you want to end up with, but what makes great wine is obviously great fruit," says Denis. "We believe wine begins in the vineyard, so we call ourselves wine growers rather than winemakers."

To that end, the team at Yamhill has experimented with a range of grape clones, along with different trellis types, barrel sources, fermentation techniques, and various ways of handling the fruit. The fruit is handled as gently as possible, so that tannins are not inadvertently extracted from the skins. Fruit ripens a little later at Yamhill than in many other vineyards in the Willamette Valley and harvest typically begins in October and lasts about two weeks.

Yamhill's team focuses on pinot blanc, pinot gris, and pinot noir, and has also transitioned to add chardonnay, as they firmly believe it will be the next great wine from Oregon. The vineyards produce an average of 250 tons of fruit each year, resulting in as much as 15,000 cases of wine annually. All stages of winemaking take place on the property, from grape growing to crush, bottling, and sales.

Top: Owner Denis Burger.
Photograph by Andréa Johnson

Middle: Owner Elaine McCall.
Photograph by Stephen J. Cary

Bottom: Stephen Cary serves as winemaker.
Photograph by Linda Arnold

Facing Page: Jenny Burger and assistant winemaker Ariel Eberle follow the vineyard guide dog, Indy.
Photograph by Andréa Johnson

Yamhill is very much a family-oriented place. Denis and Elaine's children have all worked the crush at harvest. Daughter Jenny is part of the winemaking team and son Greg serves as national sales and marketing manager. Everyone participates in hosting special events, festivals, and wine tastings. After eight years as winemaker, Denis handed over the reins to Stephen Cary, but he still manages the winery business on a daily basis. Both Denis and Elaine plan to step aside in favor of the next generation when the time is right.

In the interim, it's business as usual at Yamhill. Traditions must be observed, like an all-hands Minnesota fried chicken dinner that takes place in the middle of crush and a New England lobster feed for the entire staff at the end. And a barrel cave will become the newest addition, providing underground barrel storage and freeing up space in the winery. All the more room for continued camaraderie, winemaking, and sunset views at Yamhill Valley Vineyards.

Above: The pot of gold: Yamhill's Rainbow Vineyard.
Photograph by Stephen J. Cary

Left: Stately Oregon oaks welcome visitors to the winery.
Photograph by Stephen J. Cary

Facing Page: The winery glows warmly at night.
Photograph by Stephen J. Cary

Pinot Noir Estate
Pairs well with Traeger-grilled black-pepper rib eye steak.

Pinot Noir Reserve
Delicious when served with Mexican chicken mole.

Pinot Gris
Pairs with Panang Thai curry.

Pinot Blanc
Excellent served with oysters on the half shell.

Chardonnay
Best accompanied with halibut poached with capers.

Tastings
Open to the public daily

Yamhill Valley
vineyards

Youngberg Hill Vineyards

McMinnville

One taste of Youngberg Hill Vineyards' pinot noir and winemaker Wayne Bailey's passion is unmistakable. With the heart of a farmer and the meticulous character of an engineer, Wayne is driven by the ideals of sustainable harvesting, hard work, and a look toward the future. The result is a portfolio of wine that comes straight from nature.

Nestled among the coastal foothills of the Willamette Valley, just 25 miles from the Pacific Ocean, Youngberg Hill benefits from slightly more rainfall than much of the valley. Cool, sunny summer days and marine sedimentary and volcanic soils create berries with great acidity and an intense complexity that rival those of the Old World. The biodynamic vineyards are certified LIVE sustainable and Salmon-Safe. Taking things to the next level, Wayne evolved the biodynamic approach into a complete holistic farming practice to be in balance with nature. Rather than wait for problems to emerge, proactive and preventative measures are taken to care for the vineyard, ensuring that the vines are healthy every day of the year. Students from Oregon State and Linfield universities are invited to study the vineyards for their own research, which is also used as a way to monitor insect and avian populations that impact the crop.

Named for Wayne and Nicolette's three young daughters, the Jordan, Natasha, and Aspen blocks yield grapes that make wines as dynamic as the girls they're named for. A full-bodied wine, the Jordan Pinot Noir benefits from grapes grown on a steep slope caressed with coastal breezes on that volcanic soil. Notes of black cherry, currant, and cassis are augmented by hints of smoke and black pepper. A full texture finishes the wine, making it delicious when paired with fine cuisine or enjoyable on its own.

Top: Nicolette and Wayne Bailey stand on their front porch.
Photograph by Theresa McKeegan

Bottom: Seven-year-old Aspen Bailey helps out at harvest.
Photograph by Andréa Johnson

Facing Page: There is no shortage of great views from Youngberg Hill. Dale and Holly are on watch.
Photograph by Andréa Johnson

The dark ruby-red Natasha Pinot Noir gifts the taste buds with aromas of raspberry, rhubarb, and cherry pie. A vivacious palate of fresh berries and approachable tannins finishes with a satisfying acidity.

Aspen Pinot Gris's bright aromas of mango, grapefruit, and apricot lead to a palate of citrus and tropical fruit. The temperate Oregon summer is apparent in each sip of this stainless steel fermented wine.

Visitors enjoy the laid-back nature of the Youngberg Hill experience—sipping wine on the breezy porch while looking out over the vineyards with Mount Hood and Mount Jefferson in the distance. Guests get to know Wayne personally when they visit the tasting room, where relaxing conversation, easy laughter, and good wine are in abundance.

Above: The view from the hill is breathtaking as the morning fog rolls through the valley.

Top Left: Aspen plays on the rope swing at the top of the Jordan Block.

Bottom Left: The couple steals a kiss during a drive through the vineyard.

Facing Page: From the Martini Suite balcony at the property's inn, views of the deck and morning fog can be enjoyed.
Photographs by Andrèa Johnson

WINE & FARE

Jordan Pinot Noir
Pairs beautifully with grilled flank steak and wild mushroom risotto.

Natasha Pinot Noir
Perfect alongside pork tenderloin and mixed green salad.

Aspen Pinot Noir
Serve with smoked Brie, fresh fruit, and bread with light virgin olive oil.

Pinot Blanc
Pairs elegantly with crab cakes and grilled asparagus.

Tastings
Open to the public daily

EST. 1989

YOUNGBERG HILL

Oregon Pinot Noir
WILLAMETTE VALLEY

Z'IVO Wines

Eola-Amity Hills AVA

For John and Kathy Zelko, owners of Z'IVO Wines, it wasn't the wine country that compelled them to move from Hawaii to Oregon in 1983. It was Ken Kesey's novel, *Sometimes a Great Notion*. The book's characters were their kind of folks: living in the promising frontier of Oregon, a state that John describes as fresh and cool, with a hint of craziness. It wasn't long before the Zelkos fell in love with Oregon wine, trying every bottle they could get their hands on. They even became part-time "cellar rats" for their dear friend Rachel Starr, learning to make wine along the way. After making some amateur wine of their own, John and Kathy decided that they wanted a piece of Oregon for themselves.

A play on the Slavic word meaning "vibrant" and the diminutive form of Ivan—the Slavic version of John's name— Z'IVO can mean "Johnny's vibrant wines." These wines come from a 40-acre rocky hillside parcel in the northern tip of the Eola-Amity Hills AVA, purchased by the Zelkos in 1995 and planted in 1996.

LIVE certified and soon to be fully certified organic, the Z'IVO vineyard is farmed simply and carefully. Five separate clones of the pinot noir grape, planted in six separate micro-environments, allow for continuous fine-tuning in small-lot fermentations. The dark red, cherry, and spice-scented 2008 Eola-Amity Hills Estate Vineyard pinot noir received 93 points from *Wine Spectator* magazine and was rated as a 90-plus wine by Robert Parker's *The Wine Advocate*. The highly structured pinot blanc, produced from the very rare pinot gouges clone, is full of zesty citrus flavors, making it a beautiful accompaniment to Pacific Northwest seafood.

Top: John and Kathy Zelko have always reveled in the "industrial" side of winemaking, merging art, craft, science, and big equipment.

Bottom: Every cluster is a voice, waiting to be sung in unison.

Facing Page: The wine is showcased with a well-used Swiss Army pocketknife, purchased in Zurich solely for its corkscrew in 1972.
Photographs by Andréa Johnson

For the last 11 years, Z'IVO's award-winning portfolio of wines was produced at Walnut City Wine Works, a consortium facility in McMinnville that houses six different wineries under one roof and is symbolic of the collaborative spirit of the region. As we go to press, Z'IVO is planning an expansion to another facility that will provide an equally welcoming place for wine fans and fanatics alike to indulge their love of elegant Oregon wines.

Above: John and Kathy feel that nothing in the world could be better than hanging out in their own vineyard on a summer day with a bottle of their own wine.
Photograph by Andréa Johnson

Left: Life in full circle: Grapes are harvested at the end of the season, beginning a new vintage.
Photograph by David Farris

Facing Page: Wine is the most social of drink. It is always best with friends and family.
Photograph by Andréa Johnson

Z'IVO Whole Cluster Pinot Noir, Eola-Amity Hills
Pairs well with Northwest mushroom risotto or duck confit.

Z'IVO Estate Vineyard Pinot Noir, Eola-Amity Hills
Pairs elegantly with planked fire-roasted Chinook salmon.

Z'IVO Pinot Blanc, Eola-Amity Hills
Perfect alongside fresh oysters or fried razor clams.

Tastings
Open by appointment only

Z'IVO
W I N E S

Distinctive Destinations, page 263

McMenamins Hotel Oregon, page 269

Crawford Beck Vineyard, page 261

Lazy River Vineyard, page 267

The Allison Inn
& Spa, Willamette Valley
Newberg

Nestled among vineyards, orchards, and rich farmland, The Allison Inn & Spa is a luxurious destination resort located on 35 acres in the Willamette Valley. With more than 200 wineries nearby, many of which have tasting rooms, The Allison is a favorite among travelers who wish to immerse themselves in Oregon wine country. Seventy-seven deluxe guest rooms and eight suites welcome guests to the inn, which boasts sweeping views from private terraces and balconies. Rooms include a fireplace for romantic in-room evenings and feature a customized sliding panel beside the soaking tub that allows guests to luxuriate in a hot bath while sipping their new favorite pinot noir.

The contemporary resort is utterly timeless, with polished wood, copper accents, glass, steel, and stone on the exterior, and classically elegant, warm furnishings, handcrafted Oregon wood, and original artwork from local artisans inside. The Allison reflects the wine industry's dedication to sustainability by achieving the stringent LEED Gold certification. It's one of a handful of hotel properties that can boast such certification. Eco-friendly features include solar-powered water heaters. As a complement to the inn's sustainable practices and as a nod to the wine country itself, reclaimed wine bottles from the inn's Jory restaurant are used to craft handmade glass candles that are sold in the spa.

Top: The Allison's signature restaurant, Jory, features Oregon Wine Country cuisine.
Photograph by Barbara Kraft

Middle: Each of the resort's 77 spacious guest rooms and eight suites are complete with spa-like bathrooms, window seats, oversized windows, fireplaces, original artwork, and more.
Photograph by Barbara Kraft

Bottom: The luxurious Allison Spa has 12 treatment rooms, a fitness studio, indoor swimming pool with terrace, hair and nail salon, and a retail boutique.
Photograph by Barbara Kraft

Facing Page: Guests enjoy The Allison's fragrantly elegant gardens and pathways that connect to seven acres of vineyards and outdoor venues.
Photograph by Andréa Johnson

Jory is the inn's signature restaurant that showcases Oregon's acclaimed wines and bounteous agriculture. The restaurant's open kitchen and counter seating complement Jory's garden-to-table philosophy. Its extensive wine list has made Jory a recipient of awards from industry publications including the Best of Award of Excellence from *Wine Spectator*. Diners may select an exquisite Oregon pinot noir or limited distribution wines with cult followings as a complement to their gourmet meal.

The Allison Spa offers organic spa products and signature treatments in its private suite, 12 treatment rooms, and various lounges. From body wraps, facials, and massage treatments to a swim in the pool or a personal training session at the fitness studio, the spa is the perfect place to be pampered between vineyard walks and winery tours.

Among its diverse offerings, The Allison Inn & Spa boasts an on-site catering manager ready to assist in the planning of beautiful wine country weddings. The inn also offers ample room for corporate events. Ranked as the top hotel in the Pacific Northwest by *Condé Nast Traveler*, The Allison Inn & Spa has something for everyone.

Above: Awarded the prestigious LEED Gold Certification shortly after opening. The Allison blends naturally into the lush beauty of the area with minimal impact.

Facing Page: Hotel guests looking to explore the Willamette Valley can utilize complimentary access to The Allison's five Lexus vehicles year-round.
Photographs by Andréa Johnson

ART Elements Gallery
Newberg

Born and raised in Newberg, Loni Parrish takes great pride in preserving the town's past by giving it new life. Nowhere is that more apparent than at ART Elements Gallery in historic downtown Newberg, the gateway to the wine country. Housed in a modern-style 1940s building that Loni lovingly restored—it was an appliance shop when she was a little girl— ART Elements is dedicated to promoting local and regional artists throughout Oregon. Loni's mission is to simply create marketing opportunities for artists and to build relationships with the community and clients that ultimately enrich the lives of everyone.

Within her gallery, you'll discover a diverse collection of contemporary, modern, and impressionistic artwork, including paintings, ceramics, woodwork, sculpture, glass, drawings, photography, and jewelry from more than 60 Oregon artists. Each piece exhibits the authentic style of the region's artisans, as the art effortlessly captures emotions through color and texture. Loni, who has a degree in fine arts from Oregon State University, has since developed an acclaimed design aesthetic of her own.

What sets ART Elements apart is that it also exists beyond its walls, as Loni provides artwork consultation for private residences, businesses, and nonprofits throughout the Willamette Valley. Artwork from the gallery can be seen in select wineries of the 250 located within a 15-mile radius of downtown Newberg. Clients can also meet with the artists to understand their work better during the monthly receptions, and in many cases, Loni arranges visits to the artists' studios for a more intimate discussion. Her goal is always to expose people to art by sharing it with them. For her, a connection to the arts rounds out life and makes it even more meaningful and fulfilling.

Top: Art lover, artist, curator, and gallery owner Loni Parrish sits among the Art of The Allison artwork as it was acquired before curating the 500-piece private collection.
Photograph by Michael Wilhelm

Middle: "Poppy Lane" by nationally renowned artist Romona Youngquist, who exhibits exclusively in Oregon at ART Elements.
Photograph by Romona Youngquist

Bottom: In addition to the gallery in downtown Newberg, ART Elements Gallery also curates off-site shows and exhibitions. Jennifer Frei and David Corio's "Shapely II" was featured at the 2013 Art of The Allison Sculpture show.
Photograph by Lauren Wylie

Facing Page: Bringing art and culture to the downtown Newberg scene, ART Elements Gallery is a hub of creative activity.
Photograph by Michael Wilhelm

Loni, along with her family, curated the private collection at Newberg's Allison Inn & Spa in 2009. Which features more than 100 Oregon artists and 500 works of original art and proves her family has a long tradition of supporting the arts in their home state. It is this love of art and commitment to their community that drove the Art of The Allison Collection. Each of the 85 suites has at least three pieces of original art, and 37 paintings, sculptures, and glass are available for the public to enjoy, in addition to a substantial collection in the spa.

In 2013 the first Art of The Allison Outdoor Sculpture Show débuted, showcasing 20 fine art sculptors from the Pacific Northwest. This annual event will become a cornerstone in the foundation of the Oregon art scene in wine country. It is just another example of how all of her endeavors go back to the belief that art should be shared to enrich and invigorate community in a positive way.

Top: ART Elements Gallery hosts monthly featured artist receptions, offering the public a chance to meet the artists and learn about the creative processes, as shown with Marilyn Higginson's exhibit.

Bottom: The upper level of ART Elements Gallery's 3,000-square-foot gallery features a more intimate area for conversations, art talks, and private consultations.
Photographs by Andréa Johnson

Crawford Beck Vineyard

Amity

Jeanne and David Beck traveled all over the world chasing various wines and grapes, so when it came time to pursue the next phase of their career, wine was an obvious choice. Former scientists by profession, the couple jokingly acknowledges they went from a small laboratory to a large one, by way of the 48-acre farm on which Crawford Beck Vineyard resides. There, they grow ultra-premium fruit for chardonnay, pinot gris, and pinot noir wines.

Maintaining an ecologically balanced farm is of great important to the Becks, whose vineyard is LIVE certified sustainable. Modern agriculture requires a tremendous amount of scientific knowledge to do it well, and David feels that running a vineyard is very much like the rest of the agricultural world in that regard.

Nestled into Oregon's Willamette Valley, the 15-acre Crawford Beck Vineyard is situated in the Eola-Amity Hills, has a unique terrain with soils derived from volcanic lava and ancient marine sediment, and is cooled by the summer breezes coming through a gap in the coast range known as the Van Duzer Pass. "The various blocks of grapes are each in very different micro-environments," explains David. "The vineyard is a 'terroirist's heaven.'"

While he and Jeanne continue to look for more ways to farm their land and vineyard responsibly, they are also planning the addition of new vines to enrich what they found and make it even better.

Top: The vineyard's soils are an overlay of volcanic debris on parent material of ancient marine sediment, which dramatically influences the flavors in the grapes.
Photograph by Andréa Johnson

Middle: So strong is the Becks' commitment to sustainable farming that the vineyard was recognized with an award from their certifying organization.
Photograph by Andréa Johnson

Bottom: A perfect cluster of pinot gris grapes just before harvest is emblematic of the beauty that underlies life in the vineyard.
Photograph by David Beck

Facing Page: The Crawford Beck Vineyard lies quietly in the early morning sun, just before harvest, on the slopes of the Eola-Amity Hills.
Photograph by Andréa Johnson

Distinctive Destinations

Newberg

Newberg native Loni Parrish has traveled around the world with her family. While she has seen some amazing things, her fondest memories of traveling involve unique and meaningful experiences she shared with family and friends. With that in mind, she created Distinctive Destinations, a business that offers three exceptional and unique vacation homes in Oregon's wine country. All three of her properties are personally designed to comfortably welcome guests home, so they can make memories that will last a lifetime.

Lions Gate is a two-story 1911 Craftsman-style home located in Newberg's historical district next door to the Chehalem Cultural Center and conveniently close to a vast selection of the region's 200-plus wineries. Within walking distance to fine restaurants, tasting rooms, galleries, and boutiques, Lions Gate is the perfect location for four couples to gather for a weekend of fun and friendship. Large families can also enjoy the inviting atmosphere, as the property accommodates eight to 10 people in four suites with private baths.

Lions Gate's large backyard with beautiful gardens and an outdoor living area make it ideal for private events. Paired with the Chehalem Cultural Center, it is the perfect place for wedding parties, rehearsal dinners, and accommodations for families and friends.

Vineyard Ridge offers a vastly different experience, as the vacation home sits comfortably among the vineyards at the top of the Dundee Red Hills. The exclusive getaway, complete with a peaceful water feature flowing through the yard, accommodates four guests. A short drive down the hill and you can dine with area vintners at their local hangouts, which happen to be some of the area's finest restaurants. Should you choose to dine alfresco, however, the home's greatest offering is its breathtaking view of the Willamette Valley.

Top: Lovingly restored, Lions Gate offers guests a trip back in time to the rich designs of handcrafted homes of the turn of the century.
Photograph by Jessica Wolfer Studio

Middle: Vineyard Ridge is a modernized split-level home with Asian influences throughout, including a Zen-like garden terrace and koi pond.
Photograph by Jessica Wolfer Studio

Bottom: Suspended over the water, listening to the wind in the willows, relax in your own private retreat at the Lake House and contemplate the day's activities.
Photograph by Lauren Wylie Studio

Facing Page: Lions Gate provides the perfect home for families and friends to come together for the holidays in one warm, inviting space.
Photograph by Andréa Johnson

For a more quiet, secluded experience, there's the Lake House, or the Secret House, as it's affectionately known by locals. The Lake House rests within Yamhill County's magnificent wine country and offers the perfect getaway retreat. Its serene environment includes three and a half acres of playing ground, a small lake, three large bedrooms, two full baths, and two half baths, and it can house up to three couples.

Detailed decorating, luxury linens, and gourmet kitchens are staples in these wonderfully appointed homes. While each property has a different take on the wine country, they all offer the opportunity to experience a vacation like never before. And for Loni and her family, that is what traveling is all about.

Above: A private mystical retreat, the Lake House allows you to escape, yet is just eight miles from the burgeoning wine district of Carlton.
Photograph by Andréa Johnson

Left: Create your own special meals at Vineyard Ridge using fresh produce and fare from local farmers markets, paired with a bottle of wine from your afternoon adventure.
Photograph by Michael Wilhelm

Facing Page Bottom: Immerse yourself in the wine scene while staying at Vineyard Ridge, located on top of the famous Dundee Hills, amid the vineyards. Rub elbows with vintners in the downtown haunts.
Photograph by Michael Wilhelm

Lazy River Vineyard

Yamhill

On a picturesque fall day in 1999, a curious Streeter Roy joined his new neighbors Kirsten and Ned Lumpkin at the Yamhill, Oregon, site of what would be the Lumpkins' future vineyard. A consultant was testing the land and found prime grape-growing Jory soil. The cows in the adjacent pasture were Streeter's—so was the '53 Chevy truck bearing a large hand-painted sign that read "Lazy River Ranch." Perhaps it was kismet that one of the couple's favorite jazz songs is "Up a Lazy River." The name of their vineyard was realized.

Lazy River Vineyard is a culmination of a lifelong dream that dates back more than 50 years to when Ned was in the US Army, stationed near Frankfurt, Germany, and the famous Rheingau wine region. While there, he pooled funds with friends to taste a range of varietals, which launched his affinity for wine and special fondness for riesling.

Kirsten, a writer, and Ned, the former president of Lumpkin Construction, actually began pursuing their passion in the mid-1960s when they ventured out—"with a Volkswagen bug and a baby"—seeking vineyard property in the Yakima area of Washington state. A second foray to Walla Walla in the early '70s found no land for sale. Finally they fell in love with a parcel of land in 1999, when they found Lazy River's 146 acres of sublime, mixed terrain that is ironically punctuated by a meandering small river. One year later, they had planted their hillside with pinot noir, later adding small tracts of pinot gris and riesling.

Kirsten and Ned, along with winemaker Robert Brittan, concentrate on emboldening the flavor of the grape to yield supple and complex wines. Another emphasis at Lazy River is selling their high-quality fruit to other esteemed winemakers, including Alexana, Hamacher, Panther Creek, and Ponzi. Together with Eric Hamacher and fellow vintner Luisa Ponzi, the Lumpkins are also partners in The Carlton Winemakers Studio.

Top: A satisfying moment, as the last load of pinot noir is ready for delivery. The dogs are Moosie, a chocolate Lab, and Mario, a Lagotto Romagnola, with vineyard owners Ned and Kirsten Lumpkin.

Middle: Clusters of Wädenswil, a pinot noir clone, hang in abundance. In 2012, they were grafted onto 12-year-old rootstock and were bearing fruit for the first time.

Bottom: The vineyard's truck, a 1951 Dodge flatbed with the Lazy River logo, is a favorite of the Lumpkin family and works only during harvest.

Facing Page: One of the many great views.
Photographs by Andréa Johnson

McMenamins
Hotel Oregon

McMinnville

On McMinnville's historic main street, McMenamins Hotel Oregon strikes an inviting pose; as it has since 1905. Once home to charmers such as a soda fountain and beauty parlor, the handsome four-story building is scenically situated in Oregon's Willamette Valley, now a leading wine region with more than 200 wineries.

The Hotel's legendary Rooftop Bar offers an unobstructed, 360-degree view of the region. Once you've oriented yourself, take a spectacular seat—indoors or out—and consult an extensive wine list while you map your plan in search of Oregon's perfect pinot noir nearby.

McMenamins Hotel Oregon has 42 rooms, each with historical significance, offering visitors a glimpse of the area's past. On the main floor, visit the pub to enjoy breakfast, lunch, dinner, or late-night dining. Be sure to stop and sip a cocktail in the '20s-style Cellar Bar, where there's also free live music on weekends.

Today, as before, McMenamins Hotel Oregon is the place to come for an overnight stay near the vineyards, a stopover on the way to the coast, or just plain Oregon exploration fun.

Top: Original artwork abounds at the McMenamins Hotel Oregon. The walls, staircases, and—look up!—even piping overhead can serve as a canvas.

Middle: Cozy hotel rooms look out over McMinnville's bustling downtown.

Bottom: The Rooftop Bar provides the best view in the Willamette Valley wine country.

Facing Page: The hotel stands tall in the heart of downtown McMinnville.
Photographs courtesy of McMenamins Hotel Oregon

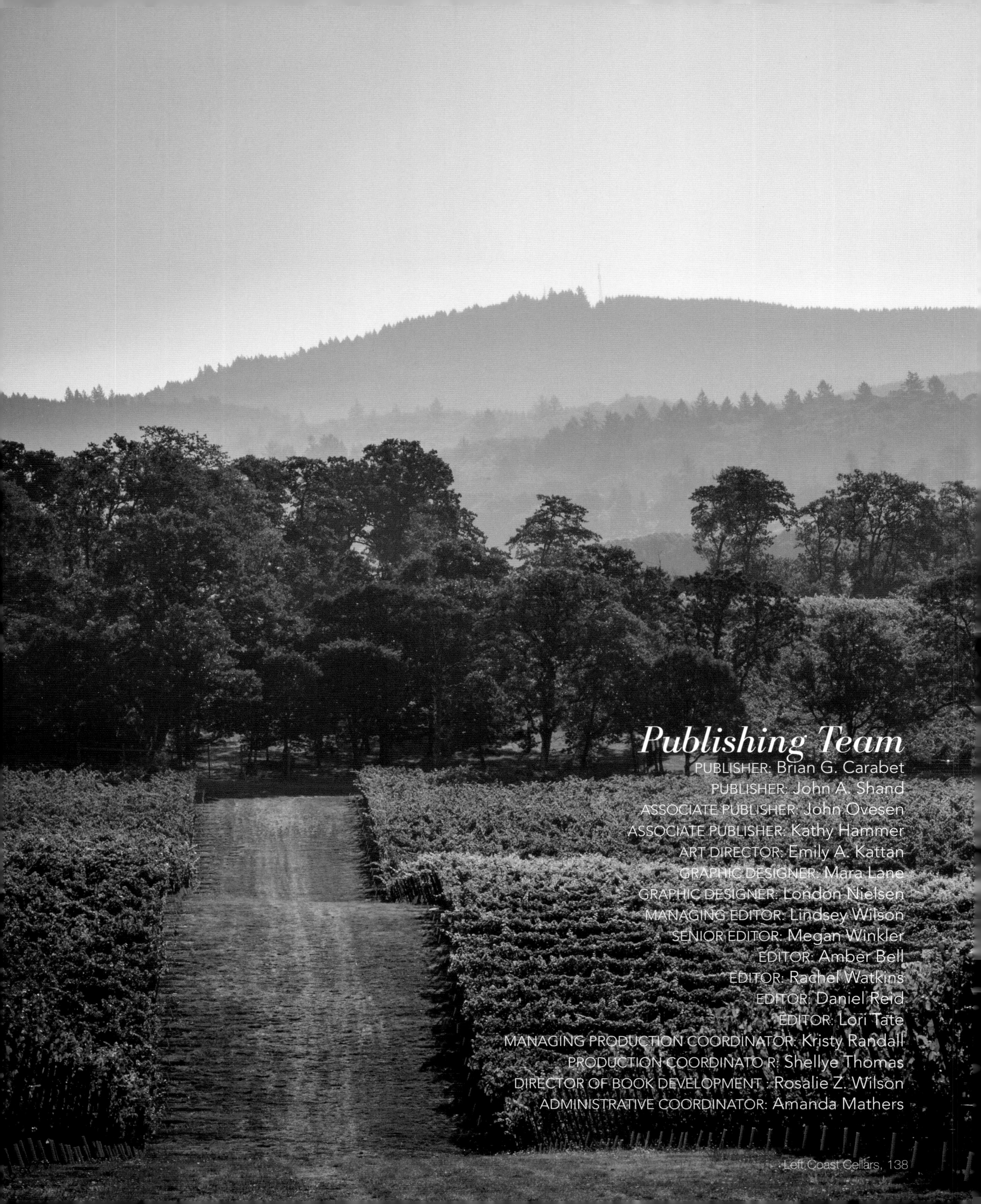

Publishing Team

PUBLISHER: Brian G. Carabet
PUBLISHER: John A. Shand
ASSOCIATE PUBLISHER: John Ovesen
ASSOCIATE PUBLISHER: Kathy Hammer
ART DIRECTOR: Emily A. Kattan
GRAPHIC DESIGNER: Mara Lane
GRAPHIC DESIGNER: London Nielsen
MANAGING EDITOR: Lindsey Wilson
SENIOR EDITOR: Megan Winkler
EDITOR: Amber Bell
EDITOR: Rachel Watkins
EDITOR: Daniel Reid
EDITOR: Lori Tate
MANAGING PRODUCTION COORDINATOR: Kristy Randall
PRODUCTION COORDINATO R: Shellye Thomas
DIRECTOR OF BOOK DEVELOPMENT : Rosalie Z. Wilson
ADMINISTRATIVE COORDINATOR: Amanda Mathers

Left Coast Cellars, 138

INDEX

THE PANACHE COLLECTION

Dream Homes Series

An Exclusive Showcase of the Finest Architects, Designers and Builders

Carolinas, Chicago, Coastal California, Colorado, Deserts, Florida, Georgia, Los Angeles, Metro New York, Michigan, Minnesota, New England, New Jersey, Northern California, Ohio & Pennsylvania, Pacific Northwest, Philadelphia, South Florida, Southwest, Tennessee, Texas, Washington, D.C., Extraordinary Homes California

Spectacular Homes Series

An Exclusive Showcase of the Finest Interior Designers

California, Carolinas, Chicago, Colorado, Florida, Georgia, Heartland, London, Michigan, Minnesota, New England, Metro New York, Ohio & Pennsylvania, Pacific Northwest, Philadelphia, South Florida, Southwest, Tennessee, Texas, Toronto, Washington, D.C., Western Canada

Perspectives on Design Series

Design Philosophies Expressed by Leading Professionals

California, Carolinas, Chicago, Colorado, Florida, Georgia, Great Lakes, London, Minnesota, New England, New York, Pacific Northwest, South Florida, Southwest, Toronto, Western Canada

Art of Celebration Series

Inspiration and Ideas from Top Event Professionals

Chicago & the Greater Midwest, Colorado, Georgia, New England, New York, Northern California, South Florida, Southern California, Southern Style, Southwest, Toronto, Washington, D.C.

City by Design Series

An Architectural Perspective

Atlanta, Charlotte, Chicago, Dallas, Denver, New York, Orlando, Phoenix, San Francisco, Texas

Spectacular Wineries Series

A Captivating Tour of Established, Estate and Boutique Wineries

California's Central Coast, Napa Valley, New York, Ontario, Oregon, Sonoma County, Texas, Washington

Experience Series

The Most Interesting Attractions, Hotels, Restaurants, and Shops

Austin & the Hill Country, British Columbia, Thompson Okanagan

Interiors Series

Leading Designers Reveal Their Most Brilliant Spaces

Florida, Midwest, New York, Southeast, Washington, D.C.

Golf Series

The Most Scenic and Challenging Golf Holes

Arizona, Colorado, Ontario, Pacific Northwest, Southeast, Texas, Western Canada

Weddings Series

Captivating Destinations and Exceptional Resources Introduced by the Finest Event Planners

Southern California

Innovative Interiors Series

Timeless To Trendsetting Commercial Interiors by Leading Architects And Designers

Carolinas, Florida, Midwest, New York, Southern California

Luxury Homes Series

High Style From the Finest Architects and Builders

Carolinas, Chicago, Florida

Specialty Titles

Publications about Architecture, Interior Design, Wine, and Hospitality

21st Century Homes, Distinguished Inns of North America, Into the Earth: A Wine Cave Renaissance, Luxurious Interiors, Napa Valley Iconic Wineries, Shades of Green Tennessee, Spectacular Hotels, Spectacular Restaurants of Texas, Visions of Design

Custom Titles

Publications by Renowned Experts and Celebrated Institutions

Cloth and Culture: Couture Creations of Ruth E. Funk, Colonial: The Tournament, Dolls Etcetera, Geoffrey Bradfield Ex Arte, Lake Highland Preparatory School: Celebrating 40 Years, Family Is All That Matters

Panache Books App

Inspiration at Your Fingertips

Download the Panache Books app in the iTunes Store to access select Panache Partners publications. Each book offers inspiration at your fingertips.

PANACHE BOOKS

Panache Partners, LLC   1424 Gables Court   Plano, Texas 75075   469.246.6060   www.panache.com